British History in P...
General Editor: Jer...

C000010563

PUBLISHED TI...

FORTHCOMING

Walter L. Arnstein *Queen Victoria*
Ian Arthurson *Henry VII*
Toby Barnard *The Kingdom of Ireland, 1640–1740*
Eugenio Biagini *Gladstone*
Peter Catterall *The Labour Party, 1918–1945*
Gregory Claeys *The French Revolution Debate in Britain*
Pauline Croft *James I*
Eveline Cruickshanks *The Glorious Revolution*
John Davis *British Politics, 1885–1939*
David Dean *Parliament and Politics in Elizabethan and Jacobean England, 1558–1614*
Colin Eldridge *The Victorians Overseas*
Richard English *The IRA*
Alan Heesom *The Anglo-Irish Union, 1800–1922*
I. G. C. Hutchison *Scottish Politics in the Twentieth Century*
Gareth Jones *Wales, 1700–1980: Crisis of Identity*
H. S. Jones *Political Thought in Nineteenth-Century Britain*
D. E. Kennedy *The English Revolution, 1642–1649*
Carol Levin *The Reign of Elizabeth I*
Roger Mason *Kingship and Tyranny? Scotland, 1513–1603*
Hiram Morgan *Ireland in the Early Modern Periphery, 1534–1690*
R. C. Nash *English Foreign Trade and the World Economy, 1600–1800*
Robin Prior and Trevor Wilson *Britain and the Impact of World War I*
Brian Quintrell *Government and Politics in Early Stuart England*
Stephen Roberts *Governance in England and Wales, 1603–1688*
David Scott *The British Civil Wars*
John Shaw *The Political History of Eighteenth-Century Scotland*
Alan Sykes *The Radical Right in Britain*
Ann Wickel *The Elizabethan Counter-Revolution*
Ann Williams *Kingship and Government in Pre-Conquest England*
Ian Wood *Churchill*

British History in Perspective
Series Standing Order
ISBN 0–333–71356–7 hardcover
ISBN 0–333–69331–0 paperback
(outside North America only)

You can receive future titles in this series as they are published by placing a standing order. Please contact your bookseller or, in case of difficulty, write to us at the address below with your name and address, the title of the series and the ISBN quoted above.

Customer Services Department, Macmillan Distribution Ltd
Houndmills, Basingstoke, Hampshire RG21 6XS, England

JOHN STUART MILL

William Stafford

Professor of Politics
University of Huddersfield

Published in Great Britain by
MACMILLAN PRESS LTD
Houndmills, Basingstoke, Hampshire RG21 6XS and London
Companies and representatives throughout the world

A catalogue record for this book is available from the British Library.

ISBN 0–333–62851–9 hardcover
ISBN 0–333–62852–7 paperback

Published in the United States of America by
ST. MARTIN'S PRESS, INC.,
Scholarly and Reference Division,
175 Fifth Avenue, New York, N.Y. 10010

ISBN 0–312–21632–7

Library of Congress Cataloging-in-Publication Data
Stafford, William.
John Stuart Mill / William Stafford.
p. cm.
Includes bibliographical references (p.   ) and index.
ISBN 0–312–21632–7
1. Mill, John Stuart, 1806–1873.   I. Title.
B1607.S73   1998
192—dc21   98–6884
                                                               CIP

This book is printed on paper suitable for recycling and made from fully managed and sustained forest sources.

10   9   8   7   6   5   4   3   2   1
07   06   05   04   03   02   01   00   99   98

Printed in Hong Kong

For Pauline

CONTENTS

INTRODUCTION

How can another book on John Stuart Mill be justified? In spite of the mountain of commentary, there are several reasons justifying a new look. First, all too often, and especially in the first century after Mill's death, interpretations have been based on a mere selection of his writings. This runs the risk of getting him wrong in all decades of his life, and is fatal for his last. Mill drafted and published no new books between 1865, when he entered parliament, and 1873 when he died; therefore any study of his big publications in isolation fails to do justice to the final evolution of his thought. For that and for the whole of his career we must turn to his letters, speeches and occasional articles. There is no excuse for ignoring these, for the Mill scholar today is blessed with a superb complete edition of thirty-three volumes: there is so much meat in it that only a dullard would be unable to find fresh perspectives.

Second, all too often Mill has been assessed anachronistically, ripped out of the context of his time. Historians of ideas are rarely guilty of this, but some philosophers and economists are. This study attempts to be fair to Mill, judging him within the parameters of what it was reasonable to think and do in the first three-quarters of the nineteenth century. But it does not regard him as of historical interest only: it frankly proposes that Mill is still exciting and relevant.

It offers a survey of Mill's reputation and of interpretations of him from his lifetime to the present, and it discusses the major areas of his thought. It differs from many interpretations in approaching not only Mill's life but also his thought as a whole as the expression of a man who was always politically engaged. It will be argued that Mill was a political animal from the crown of his hat to the sole of his boots and, in spite of what he occasionally said and of what some commentators have said about him, he was always radical. Because of his continuous political engagement, this study starts from the assumption that there is a more than usual need to have a sense of the purpose of each text, and its rhetorical strategy. Serious mistakes can be made if we assume that particular texts are full, straightforward expressions of what Mill thought. They are always tailored to an audience, an occasion, and a goal: this is true even of so 'abstract' a book as the *Logic*, as others have pointed out. Scholars are aware of this in relation to *Utilitarianism* and *On Liberty*; it is time it was recognized more fully in the case of *The Subjection of Women*.

Because of the depth of his political engagement, Mill's thought cannot be understood in a purely intellectual context, in relation to other books and authors. Mill was passionately involved in economic, social and political events, and not merely British ones: by virtue of his occupation, India (and the wider empire) was a context; he regarded himself as an expert on France and he was fascinated by America. Nor were his intellectual contexts merely British; he was immersed in French thought, aware of some German and Italian, and imaginatively absorbed in the literature of classical Greece and Rome. This study takes it for granted that any 'tunnel vision' contextualizing of Mill, relating him to a single tradition of thought, or discourse, will fail to catch him.

Since about 1970, there has been a spate of important work on Mill: general books by Robson and Ryan; collections of essays by Schneewind, Laine, and Robson & Laine; books on his philosophy by Ryan and Skorupski; on his economics by O'Brien, Hollander and Kurer; on his moral philosophy and defence of liberty by Rees, Ten, Berger, Gray and Donner; on his feminism by Tulloch and on his period in parliament by Kinzer, Robson & Robson. I write in the shadow of and in debt to this work.

In what follows, quotations from Mill have been kept to a minimum, because of constraints of length, and because of a sense that no commentary, however good, is a substitute for reading the books themselves. Mill's writings are so absorbing and eloquent that none should deny themselves the pleasures of the text.

1
LIFE AND REPUTATION

This chapter will do two things: it will set the scene by outlining the principal events of Mill's life, and it will survey the main trends in commentary and interpretation. Some interpretations will be dealt with quite briskly in this chapter: others will require fuller discussion in subsequent ones.

The Life

The standard biography is still Packe's (Packe, 1954); based on extensive research and immensely readable it is not strong on the development of ideas and occasionally slips without warning into imaginative constructions of what might have been. The principal sources for Mill's life are the thirty-three volumes of *Collected Works*, especially the *Autobiography* and the seven volumes of correspondence, which were not available when Packe wrote; they have opened a new era in Mill scholarship. Surely the twenty-first century will see a new standard life.

John Stuart Mill was born in London on 20 May, 1806. His father James Mill (1773–1836) was the son of a village shoemaker from Logie Pert, south of Aberdeen. Thanks to an ambitious mother and to the patronage of a local laird, Sir John Stuart, James Mill rose out of poverty and ignorance, gaining his degree at Edinburgh University. When his plans for a career as a Christian minister came to nothing, like many a Scot before him he migrated to London in 1802. He earned his living by his pen, as a journalist and editor; but in the year of the birth of his eldest son John Stuart, he took the risky step of giving up his editorships to rely on occasional journalism while he wrote

The History of British India. He did not finish the book until 1817, but it made both his name and his fortune. In May 1819 he was appointed Assistant Examiner of India Correspondence at India House, from which the East India Company ran the British empire in India, at the handsome salary of £800; the shoemaker's son was now firmly established as a member of the comfortable middle classes. Eventually he rose to be head of the office at a salary of £2000; John Stuart Mill joined him there in 1823, raising himself to be head of the office in 1853. Both father and son, therefore, were top 'civil servants', though working for a private company; they played a major part in ruling India though neither ever went there, neither spoke an Indian language and neither, in all probability, ever met an Indian.

But this is to anticipate. The young John Stuart Mill was educated at home by his father; it has become the most famous education of the nineteenth century. James Mill was a follower of the seventeenth-century philosopher John Locke, and of the eighteenth-century philosophers David Hartley and C.A. Helvétius. From them he had derived a belief in the enormous power of education; intelligence and virtue, he thought, were not inborn, but acquired. He therefore determined to perform an experiment on his eldest son (Stillinger, 1991, p. 23).

The boy began to learn Greek when he was three, and Latin when he was eight. In between he began mathematics, which by the age of fourteen he had taken to an advanced level. He began to read Plato in Greek when he was six or seven, by which time he had read the histories of Robertson, Hume and Gibbon and several others of similar difficulty. From the age of eight, he was given the task of supervising the lessons of his three younger brothers and five sisters – he continued to perform this duty into his thirties. He read Newton's *Principia Mathematica* when he was eleven. Beginning at the age of twelve he went through a complete course in logic and economics; he had read Adam Smith's *Wealth of Nations* and David Ricardo's *Principles of Political Economy and Taxation* before he was fourteen. By the time he was sixteen he had read some of the classics of eighteenth-century philosophy – for example, Condillac, Locke, Berkeley and Helvétius. Throughout this time he gulped huge draughts of Greek and Latin literature. Many of the books he had read by the age of sixteen would give a late twentieth-century undergraduate considerable difficulty. When he was fourteen, Mill went to France for a year; he acquired a lifelong fluency in reading, writing and speaking French, a deep love of France and a passion for botanizing.

Not only did James Mill provide his son with a better education than he could have got at any university, he also brought him into the circle of the progressive intelligentsia. Through his writing for the Whig quarterly, the *Edinburgh Review*, the father knew the editor Francis Jeffrey, and Brougham (1778–1868: Whig MP, later Lord Chancellor) and Macaulay (1800–59: Whig MP, essayist and historian). He was friendly with leading radicals – the Grotes, Austins, and Francis Place. His best friend was the economist David Ricardo (1772–1823). He brought his son into close contact with the scourge of the abuses of the legal system and father of Utilitarianism, Jeremy Bentham (1748–1832). The Mill family spent long periods amid the stately splendour of Forde Abbey in Dorset, which Bentham hired for the summer. Mill later thought that this taste of aristocratic living helped to free him from middle-class meanness and low-mindedness. He first read Bentham when he was fifteen or sixteen years old, in 1821 or 1822; he was instantly converted, becoming a utilitarian and a radical reformer. One of the issues dear to the hearts of the 'Philosophic radicals' (Mill himself coined this title for the followers of Bentham and James Mill) was population control. From the economist T.R. Malthus (1776–1834) they took the doctrine that the working masses could never become securely prosperous unless they restrained their breeding. When he was seventeen Mill wrote anonymous articles in which he advocated, in veiled language, artificial contraception (*Black Dwarf*, 27 November 1823 and 7 January 1824, *CW*, vol. XXII, pp. 82, 96). But, as the story goes, when in 1823 he distributed explicit birth control literature to servant girls he was arrested and perhaps released on bail (Schwarz, 1968, pp. 245–56); mechanical contraception was thought to be disgusting and immoral for the greater part of the nineteenth century.

In the 1820s we find Mill publishing his first articles, usually in the *Westminster Review*, the quarterly organ of the Benthamite radicals. We also find him active in the company of like-minded young men in discussion groups, and crossing swords with both Tories and Owenite socialists in debating societies: the Utilitarian Society of 1822–3, a Mutual Improvement Society of 1823–4, the Co-operative Society in 1825 and the London Debating Society 1825–9. These young Turks, Mill included, were evidently preparing themselves for political careers. Mill's close friend J.A. Roebuck became a radical MP of a somewhat intransigent type (Thomas, 1979, pp. 206–43) in 1832; but after briefly studying the law with the utilitarian legal theorist John Austin, Mill got his job at India House, which precluded parliament.

In 1826 and 1827 he undertook the crucifying task of getting Bentham's *Rationale of Judicial Evidence* ready for the press. Bentham's manuscripts are appallingly messy: the Bentham project at University College, London (which the Benthamites founded) is still working on them.

The clear, confident flow of Mill's life became troubled and diverted at the end of the 1820s and the beginning of the 1830s. Late in 1826 began his celebrated mental crisis. It may have been a depressive illness; Mill tells us that he contemplated suicide. One of his anxieties at this time was that, the notes of the scale being limited in number, all possible musical combinations would soon be exhausted. But what most troubled him, so he says, was a loss of all sense of meaning to his life. Brought up to be a reformer, in the dark autumn days of 1826 he feared that he did not care about reform, nor indeed about anything at all. His emergence from this black despair was slow, and there were relapses in 1836 (which left him with a permanent facial tic), 1843 and 1848 at least; he found consolation and a renewed sense of purpose with the help of poetry, especially Wordsworth's.

Then in 1829 came Macaulay's devastating attack on utilitarian politics in general, and on Mill's father's *Essay on Government* in particular. That essay was a textbook for the young radicals; Macaulay savaged it in the Whig *Edinburgh Review*, and the reply was published in the radical *Westminster Review*. It was a quarrel between conservative, Whig reform and radicalism which took the shape of a debate about the methods of political philosophy. The essence of utilitarianism is the moral doctrine that we ought to promote the greatest happiness of the greatest number; accordingly, James Mill argued, a good form of government would be one that did this. He combined this moral principle with the Hobbesian psychological theory that individuals or groups will tend to pursue self-interest, regardless of the common good. Therefore a monarchy, or an aristocracy, will rule in the interest of the one, or the few. The greatest happiness of the greatest number will only be promoted by a government having an interest in promoting it; it was easy for readers to conclude that the only good government would be one elected by universal suffrage. Apparently, therefore, to the horror of conservatives James Mill had provided a clear and compelling argument for democracy deduced from one moral principle and one psychological axiom. In fact James Mill himself was *not* a democrat, if by democracy is meant universal suffrage. He argued that the enfranchisement of women was unnecessary, and it is by no means clear that he was advocating universal manhood suffrage (Thomas, 1979, p. 128).

Macaulay argued that to deduce conclusions from abstract general principles in this manner was simply the wrong way to think about politics. The study of politics should be concrete and historical, not abstract and deductive. For example, as a matter of fact it was just not true that individuals and groups always ruled selfishly. Humans were not always and everywhere the same, therefore it was utterly impossible to 'deduce the science of government from the principles of human nature' (Lively & Rees, 1978, p. 124). Instead of a deductive political science, Macaulay proposed an empirical one, that is to say one based upon extensive and intimate knowledge of the historical and contemporary facts, a knowledge of the diversity of humanity. There can be no doubt that John Stuart Mill was shaken by this critique of his utilitarian heritage.

At about this time Mill became friendly with the Anglican Christians F.D. Maurice (1805–72) and John Sterling (1806–44). These men were much influenced by the thought of Coleridge, and through them Mill met the 'sage of Highgate'. Benthamism represented the spirit of the late eighteenth-century radical Enlightenment: Coleridge, having turned from poetry to philosophy was the most powerful critic of the Enlightenment, transmitting to his readers and disciples the misty and mystical philosophy of German Romanticism. Coleridge by this time was a conservative with a conscience, a Tory paternalist, but not all of his followers were conservative – F.D. Maurice was later a Christian socialist. There were further encounters with this Germanic anti-Enlightenment and indeed anti-utilitarian tendency after Mill met the writer (in due course 'Victorian sage') Thomas Carlyle (1795–1881) in 1831; they became close friends, and their friendship even survived the accidental burning of the only manuscript of the first volume of Carlyle's *French Revolution* while it was in Mill's possession. A further injection of doubts about democratic radicalism came from Mill's enthusiastic reading and reviewing of Alexis de Tocqueville's *Democracy in America* in the mid-1830s.

There were other French influences on Mill's thought at this time. He was greatly excited by the French revolution of 1830, going off to Paris with his radical young friends G.J. Graham and J.A. Roebuck. A year or so earlier he had met Gustave d'Eichthal, the socialist follower of the proto-social scientist Saint-Simon (1760–1825) at the London Debating Society; while in Paris he visited the Saint-Simonian leaders, and d'Eichthal was determined to win him for the cause. At this time the 'father of sociology' Auguste Comte (1798–1857) was still numbered among the Saint-Simonian socialists, and Mill had read and admired his *Traité de politique positive*. He studied Comte's *Cours de Philosophie Positive* from 1837 and entered into a long correspondence with Comte in 1841.

Mill's Benthamite radicalism, therefore, suffered attack from several quarters in the decade after 1826: from his own inner crisis, from Macaulay's assertion of a historical and empirical method, from the Germano-Coleridgean assault on the Enlightenment, from French socialism (and British co-operative socialism) and Comtean sociology. Under the impact of these hammer-blows he set about reconstructing his philosophy; his rebuilding work is captured in a series of brilliant articles: 'The spirit of the age' in 1831, 'Tocqueville on Democracy in America, vol. I' in 1835, 'Civilization' in 1836. While his father was alive, this dutiful son could not utter the fullness of his dissent; but James Mill died in 1836. Now Mill could write the three essays which fully stated his new position: 'Bentham' in 1838 and 'Coleridge' and 'Tocqueville on Democracy in America, vol. II' in 1840.

Also in the 1830s, Mill fell desperately in love with Harriet Taylor, an intelligent woman who belonged to a radical Unitarian circle (the Unitarians were 'rational' Christians who, in the spirit of the Enlightenment, denied the divinity of Christ). The problem was that she was already married, with three children. A crisis was reached in 1833; Mill and Harriet stayed in Paris and were evidently considering living together (*CW*, vol. XII, p. 178). The scandal would have wrecked Mill's career, and in the event conventional propriety triumphed. Fortunately the husband, John Taylor, was astonishingly noble-minded; he opened his doors to the lovesick philosopher, set up his wife in a country cottage where she and Mill could weekend together, and paid for her to take long trips abroad in Mill's company. All of this was done with care so as to avoid scandal. Even more astonishing to twentieth-century readers is the indubitable fact, proved by one of Harriet Taylor's own letters, that there was no sex; the relationship, passionate and intense, was purely Platonic.

Throughout this time Mill was working at India House. His job required attendance from 10 till 4, six days a week; but often he could clear his desk in half that time, devoting the rest to his own reading and writing. In 1830–1 he wrote his *Essays on Some Unsettled Questions of Political Economy*; though they embodied his most creative thinking as a technical economist, they were not published until 1844. In the late 1830s he was proprietor and effective editor of the *London and*

Westminster Review. Throughout the decade he was closely involved, through his journalism and editorial work, in the politics of radicalism, seeking to remould its philosophy along the lines of his own rethinking, and to organize the radicals in parliament to push the Whig government along the path of further reform. He was appalled by the declaration in 1837 of the leader of the House of Commons Lord John Russell ('Finality John') (1792–1878) that the 1832 reform settlement was definitive, and in 1838 and 1839 he advocated a progressive alliance of Whigs and radicals under Lord Durham ('Radical Jack'). But it all came to nothing. Durham (1792–1840) proved a broken reed, the radicals were hopelessly divided and hopelessly led, and the reformed electorate and House of Commons was moving away from the Whigs towards the Conservatives (Thomas, 1979, pp. 439–53). Mill refocused his efforts on research and writing.

In 1843 he published his *System of Logic*. No work ever cost him so much trouble: it took him thirteen years to write. Then in 1848 he published his *Principles of Political Economy*, having almost dashed it off; he had begun work on this massive book in the autumn of 1845. These two works provided the basis for Mill's great reputation in the nineteenth century, dominating their respective disciplines for a generation or more; the *Political Economy* went through thirty-two editions before the century ended. In the 1840s he withdrew increasingly from social life; the society of Harriet Taylor was enough. He drifted away from Carlyle, fell out with Comte because the latter insisted that women were inherently inferior to men, and with the Austins because they did not share his enthusiasm for the 1848 revolution in Paris.

In 1849 John Taylor died, and in 1851 Mill and Harriet married. Their happiness was soon alloyed. Mill was suffering from tuberculosis; a year after their marriage, Harriet exhibited symptoms of the disease. Mill's father and his dear friend John Sterling had died of it: it was to kill two of his brothers. By 1854 he and his wife were expecting, with good reason, that they would die within a year. Attempting to secure a respite, in 1854–5 Mill toured, often on foot, in Italy, Sicily and Greece; he returned, miraculously, on the mend. He wanted to live a little longer, because he believed he had a great task to perform. He sincerely thought that his wife was the truly creative thinker; his mission was to present her ideas to the world. Therefore they set to work to write drafts containing the essence of their thought, as a legacy to posterity. She had already played a part in revising the *Political Economy*; now they drafted the essay *On Liberty* and the *Autobiography*, and essays on nature, Utilitarianism and religion. In 1851, Mill had published under his own name an essay on the 'Enfranchisement of Women' calling for votes for women and access to jobs and careers; later he insisted that the essay had been written by his wife. In his introduction to the first reprinting of it in 1859, Mill penned the most extravagant eulogy: she had 'a mind and heart which in their union of the rarest, and what are deemed the most conflicting excellences, were unparalleled in any human being that I have known or read of... I venture to prophecy that if mankind continue to improve, their spiritual history for ages to come will be the progressive working out of her thoughts, and realization of her conceptions' (*CW*, vol. XXI, p. 394). In 1858, in the aftermath of the Indian Mutiny, the East India Company was wound up, and its functions transferred to the British state. Mill was pensioned off at three-quarters salary – £1500 per year. He was free, and at the end of the year he and Harriet set off for southern Europe. She was taken ill and died of TB quite suddenly at Avignon. Mill was devastated: 'The spring of my life is broken' (*CW*, vol. XV, p. 574). He buried her in the Protestant cemetery on the outskirts of the city, and bought a house, 'Monloisir' within sight of it, where henceforth he lived for a part of the year. He raised a costly marble tomb, which he visited every day, lovingly tending the garden round about it; as he expressed it, atheist that he was, 'Her memory is to me a religion' (*CW,* vol. I, p. 251). His stepdaughter Helen Taylor now became his constant and devoted companion; she was as intellectual and as fiercely radical as her mother, and was to him 'another such prize in the lottery of life' (*CW,* vol. I, p. 264).

Mill had published little new work for ten years; after Harriet Mill's death there came a series of important books which, in Mill's own estimation, brought him a wider celebrity than his massive treatises on logic and political economy had obtained (*CW*, vol. XV, p. 843). The essay *On Liberty*, which he claimed was a joint work in which all the best thoughts came from his wife, came out immediately in 1859, followed by *Considerations on Representative Government* in 1861 and *Utilitarianism* in 1863. In the period subsequent to their friendship, Auguste Comte had published his *Système de Philosophie Positive* in which his traditional attitudes on the women question, and also his authoritarianism, became more apparent. Comte called for a dictatorship by scientific experts, the end of free thought and the burning of dissentient books. In 1865 Mill settled accounts with him in *Auguste Comte and Positivism*. In the same year he returned to pure philosophy with *An Examination of Sir William Hamilton's Philosophy* – in reality as much a demolition as an examination. This was the book in which he made his celebrated reply to those Christians who argued that acts of God which appear evil by our standards are not really evil; we must have faith in God's goodness: 'I will call no being good who is not what I mean when I apply that epithet to my fellow-creatures; and if such a creature can sentence me to hell for not so calling him, to hell I will go' (*CW*, vol. IX, p. 103). Many, including Christians, thought that Mill was right: but he was denounced in one newspaper as 'chief of the Satanic School in England' (Packe, 1954, p. 444).

Mill turned back at this time to active politics. He wrote with passion and urgency, against the tide of middle and upper-class opinion in England, to support the Northern side in the American Civil War; to Mill it was not a battle against agreeable Southern gentlemen of the 'gone with the wind' kind but a crusade against slavery. After his wife's death he became more sociable, and collected a group of allies, admirers and disciples – the philosophers Herbert Spencer and Alexander Bain, the economist J.E. Cairnes, the politician and writer John Morley, the liberal politician Henry Fawcett and his wife Millicent Garrett Fawcett who was later to be a leading campaigner for women's suffrage. He and Helen Taylor became close friends with Lord John Russell's son, Lord Amberley, and his wife, and later stood as godparents for their son, Bertrand Russell. He also maintained contact with working-class politicians and co-operators. Mill had achieved a formidable reputation as a thinker and was now a leading light in advanced liberal circles. It was therefore natural that he should be invited to stand for the radical constituency of Westminster in 1865. Mill took the opportunity offered by his enhanced prominence to bring out several of his works in cheap popular editions; in order to get the prices as low as possible, he agreed to forgo his royalties. This tells us something about Mill's perception of himself as a prophet or missionary for advanced liberalism; and apparently the People's Editions did no harm to the full-price sales (*CW*, vol. XVI, p. 1060). Mill was elected as MP for Westminster, and subsequently as rector of St Andrews University; his inaugural address in 1867 – 'a very lengthened performance; its delivery lasted three hours' (Bain, 1882, p. 126) – defended a broad curriculum based on the sciences and humanities rather than practical subjects.

While in parliament, Mill largely supported the liberal leader Gladstone, for whom at this time he had considerable admiration. He moved an amendment to Disraeli's reform bill to admit women to the franchise on the same terms as men; it lost but received 80 votes.

He spoke out for a lenient and conciliatory policy towards Ireland in spite of Fenian terrorism, and for Irish land reform. His most unpopular stand was over the Eyre case. Eyre, Governor of Jamaica, had put down a revolt with considerable brutality and some illegality. For Mill it was not enough that Eyre had been dismissed; he should be brought to trial for murder. Mill's principled stand brought him abusive letters and a death-threat.

After the passing of Disraeli's 1867 Reform Act, there was a general election with the newly enlarged electorate, and Mill was defeated. He was genuinely pleased to be free again, preferring as he did Avignon to Westminster – 'It is an infinitely pleasanter mode of spending May to read the *Gorgias* and *Theatetus* under the avenue of mulberries … surrounded by roses and nightingales' (*CW*, vol. XVI, p. 1060) – but his political activities did not cease. With Helen Taylor he continued to be active in the campaign for women's suffrage and he appeared before the Royal Commission on the Contagious Diseases Acts, which authorized the medical inspection and detention of prostitutes in certain garrison towns, to argue the feminist case for their repeal. In 1869 he judged that the time was ripe to bring out his essay on *The Subjection of Women* – it had been ready since 1861. He became active in the Land Tenure Reform Association, which favoured a measure of land nationalization. But he was happy to spend much of his time at Avignon with Helen Taylor, and it was here in 1873, after a pleasant long walk botanizing in the Vaucluse, that he contracted erysipelas (a fever with inflammation of the skin) and died in three days. In 1854, when he had thought he was dying of consumption, he had written 'I seem to have frittered away the working years of life in mere preparatory trifles, and now "the night when no one can work" has surprised me with the real duty of my life undone' (*CW*, vol. XXVI, p. 665). Now his final words to Helen were 'You know I have done my work'. She brought out his last works posthumously: the *Autobiography* in 1873, *Three Essays on Religion* in 1874 and the unfinished *Chapters on Socialism* in 1879. Mill lies, as he wished, in Avignon under the marble tomb beside Harriet.

The Reputation

The literature of commentary on John Stuart Mill is now immense. Controversies about the correct interpretation and assessment of him and his books are legion; here I can notice only the main trends.

Mill's reputation was already controversial during his life. Initially this was because Utilitarianism itself was controversial: literary figures such as Coleridge in *The Friend*, Carlyle in *Past and Present* and Dickens in *Hard Times*, looking from the standpoint of the romantic imagination, castigated Utilitarianism as hard, heartless, mechanical, philistine, godless and base. Mill was receptive to these criticisms; his essay on *Utilitarianism* was a brilliant rescue-operation which showed that it could be as noble and inspiring as any other morality. He made it both publicly and academically respectable as, at the very least, a plausible and discussable theory of morality, a position it has retained ever since (Schneewind, 1976, pp. 35–52). He also redeemed political economy from its reputation as the 'dismal science' and in the second half of the nineteenth century his influence on young men in the universities was enormous: T.H. Green, the Oxford idealist philosopher is said to have murmured on his deathbed in 1882, 'Mill was such a *good* man' (Harvie, 1976, pp. 38, 151). In the last decade of his life, and especially from the time of his parliamentary candidature, controversy about him widened and intensified; the rapturous reception he received at public meetings on the one hand, and on the other his vilification by the conservative press, testify to this. In addition to the political stances he adopted, which will be considered later, his essays *On Liberty* and *The Subjection of Women* provoked both enthusiasm and hostility. His critics found subversive subtexts: they thought that his barely concealed aims were to subvert Christianity and promote divorce, thereby undermining the very foundations of society. Many thought that his doctrine of liberty, licensing individuals within wide limits to think, speak and act as they liked, was forgetful of the need to protect the coherence and identity of society as a community of belief and action. Others thought that his doctrines about women were just plain wrong: it was obvious to them that women were inferior, mentally as well as physically and that their place was in the home under the authority of their husbands (Pyle, 1994; 1995).

Immediately after his death, Mill was the victim of a sharp attack by Abraham Hayward, both in a *Times* obituary and in *Fraser's Magazine* (Hayward, 1873a; 1873b). Hayward was a conservative lawyer and Mill's contemporary; they had crossed swords in the London Debating Society in the late 1820s and Mill, then a callow Benthamite, had uttered unforgivable words. Late in 1837 or early in 1838 Hayward protested to Mill about an article in the *Westminster Review* (not in fact by Mill, but Mill was the editor) accusing Hayward and others of doing 'the base work of the aristocracy, fighting for them, writing for them, joking for them, blackguardizing for them, and...lying for them' (*CW*, vol. XIII, p. 367n). At last in 1873 Hayward had his revenge. He averred that Mill was a fanatic in the cause of human progress who did an infinity of harm; he advocated the fanciful rights of women and impracticable, revolutionary reforms in the laws relating to land; he advanced socialistic opinions under female training. Hayward also retailed the story of Mill in his teens advocating birth control, and more or less accused him of adultery with Harriet Taylor. The subsequent controversy caused Prime Minister Gladstone, who had dubbed Mill 'the saint of liberalism,' to withdraw his support for a memorial in Westminster Abbey. It is important to emphasize these events, because, looking back from the late twentieth century, it is all too easy to think of Mill as a respectable Victorian liberal and pillar of the establishment. Such a view is a misapprehension of his status and significance in and immediately after his own day.

The Victorians of the last quarter of the nineteenth century assessed Mill's significance with some ambiguity. A widely received view, proposed by Dicey, has been that the heyday of liberal individualism ended about 1870, to be followed by a gradually ascendant collectivism (Dicey, 1914, p. 432). If the fundamental discipline for Mill, as for the 'philosophic radicals' generally, was political economy, centring on that selfish individual, 'economic man', then post-1870 was the glory day of biology with its ruling ideas of organic and functional unity (Freeden, 1978, pp. 18, 93). A collectivist neo-Hegelian philosophy was increasingly influential. Mill knew the German philosopher Hegel (1770–1831) only at second hand, and he did not like what he knew: 'For some time after I had finished the book all such words as *reflexion, development, evolution*, etc., gave me a sort of sickening feeling which I have not yet entirely got rid of ' (*CW*, vol. XVI, p. 1323). Some late nineteenth-century commentators such as the neo-Hegelian philosophers Bosanquet, Bradley, Ritchie and to an extent Leslie Stephen (the historian of Utilitarianism and founding editor of the *Dictionary of National Biography*) thought that these developments had rendered Mill a yesterday's man, trapped in an individualistic paradigm belonging to the eighteenth-century Enlightenment.

This judgement was at best a caricature, at worst downright false (Freeden, 1978, pp. 23–4; Collini, 1991, p. 168). Dicey himself insisted that Mill's later teachings prepared the minds of the rising generation to accept collectivism, and he cited Stephen and the late nineteenth-century philosopher Sidgwick as authorities for the view that Mill was a socialist (Dicey, 1914, pp. 429, 432). Early Fabian socialists deep-dyed in collectivism were happy to claim Mill as a precursor. The balance of individualism and collectivism in Mill's thought remains an issue to this day and will receive attention in subsequent chapters.

Gradually it became fashionable to disparage him as second rate, unoriginal as a philosopher and economist, muddy and confused as a thinker. Bradley, writing in 1876 from a neo-Hegelian, anti-individualist standpoint, picked logical holes in Mill's utilitarianism in order to reject it altogether (Bradley, 1927, pp. 92, 112–14, 119–24). Jevons, one of the inaugurators of the 'marginalist' revolution in economics which with its mathematical approach appeared to render all previous textbooks (including Mill's) redundant, attacked both Mill's economics and his logic (Jevons, 1871; 1890). During the last quarter of the nineteenth century, these criticisms slowly made their way against Mill's prestige; by the early twentieth a consensus was emerging. It is strikingly voiced in G.E. Moore's *Principia Ethica* of 1903, which discusses Mill's *Utilitarianism*. Mill is there accused of all manner of fallacies, including 'naïve and artless' ones; his 'proof' of the principle of utility, already savaged by Bradley, came in for particular scorn: 'Well, the fallacy in this step is so obvious, that it is quite wonderful how Mill failed to see it' (Moore, 1903, pp. 66–7).

For the first half of the twentieth century this rather disparaging view was the dominant one. For example, according to his godson in 1951, Mill's *Logic* and *Principles of Political Economy* were conventional and unimportant; Mill never learnt to think in a mathematical way (Russell, 1969, pp. 1, 2, 4, 9). Plamenatz, writing in 1949 with obvious liking for Mill and a conviction that 'the study of his confusions and errors is nearly always profitable', thought that by the time of his essays *On Liberty* and *Utilitarianism*, Mill was exhausted and prematurely aged by illness, unable to keep control of his arguments. Students should read him in order 'to exercise the destructive faculties indispensable to the philosopher' (Plamenatz, 1958, pp. 123, 144). At almost the last gasp of this phase of Mill scholarship, McCloskey's lucid study, though warmly sympathetic to Mill's radicalism, finds him guilty of many errors (McCloskey, 1971).

What were the key problems identified by this critical phase of Mill scholarship, which must be discussed later? Three aspects of the essay on *Utilitarianism* drew most fire. First, it was contended that his 'proof' of the principle of utility contained a crude logical mistake. Second, his argument that only pleasure is desirable for its own sake was thought to be unconvincing and indeed incoherent. Third, it was said that his distinction between higher and lower pleasures effectively subverted Utilitarianism, though Mill himself did not realize this. Nor was it only the essay on Utilitarianism which was seen to be fraught with problems. His essay *On Liberty* has as its cornerstone the principle that individuals should not be prevented from acting, either by law or by public opinion, when their actions are purely self-regarding, affecting only themselves. This central doctrine, the keystone of Mill's liberalism, was held to be incoherent; few if any actions, it was argued, affect only the doers and are purely self-regarding (Bosanquet, 1923, pp. 60–3; Rees, 1985, p. 145). In the first half of this century, *Utilitarianism* and *On Liberty* were probably the most widely read of Mill's works, standard fare on university syllabuses in Philosophy, Politics and History. It was widely thought that the two were inconsistent. *Utilitarianism* says that we should promote the good, that is to say, happiness: *On Liberty* insists that where self-regarding acts are concerned we should not interfere with individuals *even for their own good*. One work makes happiness most important, the other liberty; one work is utilitarian, the other is not. It was argued that this contradiction ran right through Mill's philosophy, and this interpretation can still be found in recent scholarship (Anschutz, 1953; Francis & Morrow, 1994).

A variation on this theme is the contention that the contradictions in his thought reflect stages of his mental development, stages which took him in different directions, directions which he never succeeded in reconciling. The origin of this interpretation is his own *Autobiography*. There we learn that he began as an orthodox Benthamite radical, an heir of the eighteenth-century Enlightenment, who became disenchanted and turned to romantic poetry, and to the conservative anti-Enlightenment philosophies of Wordsworth, Coleridge and Carlyle. Critics saw this as the source of all his later contradictions; he continued to be torn between Bentham and Coleridge, the Enlightenment and Romanticism, iconoclasm and reverence for history, individualism and organicism, liberty and authority, radicalism and conservatism, the ethic of pleasure and the ethic of free self-expression.

The second half of the twentieth century has seen a different trend in Mill scholarship (and in the history of philosophy more generally) which might be called 'revisionist' (Gray & Smith, 1991, pp. 1–19) or more precisely *hermeneutic*. That is to say, instead of reading his texts destructively, awarding ticks and crosses as if marking an exam paper, Mill is read sympathetically, in an attempt fully to understand his arguments and intentions. Two important books by Alan Ryan established this trend (Ryan, 1970; 1974) which had begun mid-century. Its result has been the presentation of a strong case for Mill's philosophical originality, power and consistency. After all, it is inherently implausible that a man who began his training in logic at the age of twelve and who wrote a classic treatise on the subject would be guilty of elementary logical errors. Earlier critics went wrong by failing to read Mill with sufficient care, and especially by reading him selectively; his thought is never simple, and his initial statements have to be understood in the context of his later qualifications and elaborations. As Urmson wrote in 1953, 'Instead of Mill's own doctrines a travesty is discussed, so that the most common criticisms of him are simply irrelevant' (Urmson, 1969, p. 180). As has recently been said: 'Mill has adequate replies to many subsequent critics whose points often repeat those of Macaulay and seem to have continuing relevance only because those critics have failed in their scholarly duty to read Mill carefully' (Wilson, 1990, p. 19). The charge of incoherence levelled at Mill's 'one simple principle' in *On Liberty*, based on the distinction between self- and other-regarding actions, seemed incontrovertible to late nineteenth-century philosophers such as Bosanquet and Ritchie, because they were neo-Hegelians who believed that all is but part of one stupendous whole. Therefore a free-standing self uninvolved with others was at each and every moment impossible. The eclipse of Hegelianism robbed this charge of its self-evident force. It was seriously damaged in a classic article by John Rees (Rees, 1960). Alan Ryan constructed a powerful case for the overall coherence of Mill's thought, arguing that *On Liberty* could only be understood if it was read together with the whole of *Utilitarianism*, including the neglected last chapter on justice, and the last part of the *Logic*. John Gray, Fred Berger and John Skorupski, among others, have developed and strengthened this line of argument (Gray, 1983; Berger, 1984; Skorupski, 1989). The essential continuity of Mill's thought, and therefore his consistency, have been defended by Robson, Halliday, Rees and Thomas (Robson, 1968; Halliday, 1976; Rees, 1985; Thomas, 1985). His originality and power as an economist have been vindicated too (O'Brien, 1975; Stigler, 1976).

These articles and books are heavy artillery; now that they have done their work, it does not make sense to defend the view that Mill's mature work contains crude fallacies and glaring inconsistencies, and

therefore the pages that follow will largely ignore that view. For example, I shall pay no further attention to the criticisms of Mill's alleged
'proof' of the principle of utility; as Mill expressly stated, he was not
attempting to prove it, and his arguments, if read sympathetically, can
be defended (Hall, 1969, pp. 145–78; Warnock, 1969, pp. 199–203).
I am not claiming, however, that there are no tensions and difficulties
in Mill's philosophy. As we shall see, problems remain, but they are
deep problems which philosophy itself has not resolved.

Interwoven with the debate about Mill's stature as a thinker are
debates about his ideological stance. Very often the interpretations
proffered are themselves ideological, attempts to co-opt Mill for a particular political position, or to hold him up as a horror to be avoided.
Mention has already been made of the common late-nineteenth-
century interpretation of him as a socialist. This was an easier view
to hold at a time when party boundaries were fluid, when the liberal
chancellor of the exchequer Sir William Harcourt could say in 1894,
'we are all socialists now', and when Fabian socialists could think of per-
meating either liberals or conservatives (Freeden, 1978, pp. 27, 35–6,
40, 49, 150, 159). But with the emergence of an independent party of
labour around the turn of the century, new ideological boundaries
emerged. It came to seem necessary to allocate Mill either to liberalism
or to socialism, and in the twentieth century the balance of judgement
has awarded Mill to the liberals (Berlin, 1969, pp. 183–4n.; Duncan,
1973, p. 244). Socialist scholars have written of Mill with respect
(Williams, 1963, pp. 65–84; Macpherson, 1977, pp. 2, 44–70; Arblaster,
1984, pp. 278–82) but have tended to argue that, while his intentions
were good, they were vitiated by the liberal individualist framework
which he never abandoned. Yet Mill insisted he was a socialist, and now
that socialism is redefining itself after the collapse of the command
economies of Eastern Europe, the question looks thoroughly open
again. The most powerful attempt to play down Mill's socialist credentials is Hollander's two-volume study of his economics; the opposite
case has been well argued by Kurer (Hollander, 1985; Kurer, 1991).
Hollander's book has a clear agenda of a somewhat scholastic kind: he
aspires to show that all the great classical and neo-classical economists –
Adam Smith, Ricardo, Mill, and the 'marginalists' of the late nineteenth century – were in essential agreement in their defence of a
free-enterprise system. In subsequent chapters it will be necessary to
discuss both Mill's socialism and whether he was simply a follower of
Ricardo.

Of course, liberals still claim Mill for their own, and find their current concerns reflected in his thought. The reaction against collectivism after experience of European Fascism and Russian Communism brought a revival in his reputation; he became a Cold War hero. Isaiah Berlin presented Mill as an ethical pluralist like himself. According to this view Mill recognized that there was no static human nature, no final truth in human affairs and no single account of the good. Humans pursue different goods between which there is no way of judging, and which cannot be combined in a single system, capable of being enforced without violating anyone's preferred values. This is the basis of his case for the tolerance of individual diversity (Berlin, 1969, pp. 173–206). Berlin's pupil Graeme Duncan did not agree: Mill thought there were right answers to moral questions (Duncan, 1973, p. 268). More recently, John Gray has endorsed Berlin's interpretation (Gray & Smith, 1991, pp. 193, 201, 205), and this is a key issue to which we must return.

Mill's capacity to irritate conservatives has not diminished with time. In 1963 his doctrine of liberty was subjected to a vicious attack by Maurice Cowling. Cowling contended that Mill was a hypocritical liberal; the freedom he believed in was not freedom for everyone but only freedom for people like himself, for left-wing atheistic intellectuals; he was perfectly happy for the state or for society to interfere with those who did not measure up to his own standards. 'Mill was a proselytizer of genius: the ruthless denigrator of existing positions, the systematic propagator of a new moral posture, a man of sneers and smears and pervading certainty' (Cowling, 1990, p. 93). At about the same time a similar case was made with similar rudeness by Letwin, who depicted Mill as a stage on a downward slope leading from the eighteenth-century sanity and conservatism of David Hume to the Fabian socialism and collectivism of Beatrice Webb (1858–1943). Mill went astray by following alien (especially German) influences, even though he did not properly understand German Romanticism. He represents the evil of rationalism in politics, being an intolerant, elitist, puritan perfectionist, a sham liberal who wanted the government 'to impose what he considers the good life on all his fellows' (Letwin, 1965, p. 8). Cowling's and Letwin's attacks, hostile and ideologically motivated though they were, gained purchase because there is a real problem of interpretation here, which must be discussed later; to what extent did Mill qualify his doctrine of liberty with an advocacy of authority and of collective action for the good of the whole?

A very different and to some extent opposed conservative critique was offered in a provocative book by the American scholar Gertrude Himmelfarb (Himmelfarb, 1974). Her stance towards Mill is related to that strand in American conservative thinking which repudiates 'liberalism'. To such critics, the 'advanced liberalism' to which Mill explicitly gives allegiance is more akin to anarchic licence than to healthy freedom. It goes hand-in-hand with a superficial, critical rationalism lacking in respect for tradition and authority, and it dreams of an unrealistic and dangerous equality.

Variants of this critique are offered by Joseph Hamburger (Hamburger, 1976, pp. 114–24) and Willmore Kendall (Kendall, 1975, pp. 157–65). Himmelfarb's interpretation attempts to rescue at least a part of Mill's legacy from this critique. She thinks that Mill's 'conservative' phase in the 1830s represents Mill at his best – the essays on 'The spirit of the age' and 'Civilization', on de Tocqueville, Bentham and Coleridge are a marked improvement on the crudities of Benthamite Utilitarianism. This 'other' Mill was a conservative liberal who recognized that freedom had to be balanced with discipline, the demands of the individual with the needs of the community. But then in the 1840s Mill swung back to the superficialities of his youth – why? – because of Harriet Taylor, an unpleasant, dogmatic and mediocre woman: 'Yet there is no doubt of the enormity of her influence ...' (Himmelfarb, 1962, p. xix).

According to Himmelfarb, Harriet forced him against his will down the road of socialism, and away from eclectic tolerance towards radical dogmatism. She inoculated him with her passion for feminism. This was in fact the cause of the extreme and unqualified libertarianism of his essay *On Liberty*. The morality of utility does not necessarily lend support to the feminist cause; some women, perhaps most women, might be happier with traditional feminine roles. But liberty, taken as an absolute, must imply the emancipation of women. After Harriet's death, Mill moved back towards his richer and more broad-minded stance of the 1830s as, for example, his essay on *Representative Government* reveals. For Himmelfarb the essay *On Liberty* is an inferior work, its ideas akin to those which motivated the excesses of campus radicalism in the 1960s.

Some aspects of Himmelfarb's interpretation can be dismissed quite quickly. To contend that *On Liberty* is poor, an inferior work in Mill's *oeuvre*, is too unconvincing to merit discussion; it is the work on which his status as a classic has been based. To argue that after Harriet's death Mill moved back to a more conservative position will convince no-one who has read the corpus of Mill's letters and speeches in his last decade. Rather the contrary is the truth: Mill's suspicions of democracy were strongest while Harriet was alive, and later he became more radical both politically and socially, especially after his experience of conservatism in the flesh in the House of Commons (Wolfe, 1975, pp. 42, 51–60).

But important issues for discussion are raised here. First, did Mill abandon, or largely transform, his Benthamite heritage? Some have thought this greatly exaggerated, and that fundamentally Mill remained a philosophic radical (Ryan, 1974, p. 56; Thomas, 1985, pp. 33–7). They say that his apparent distance from Benthamism is apparent only because Benthamism has been caricatured, an activity of which Mill himself was sometimes guilty. Just as crude Marxism has been blamed, not on the master himself but on his disciple Engels, so the more dogmatic form of philosophic radicalism has been attributed not to the great thinkers such as Bentham and Ricardo, but to that hard and narrow man, James Mill (Hollander, 1985). Even this has been contested, and the essential continuity between the thought of father and son defended (Rees, 1985, pp. 10–50).

Second, was there a distinct conservative period in Mill's intellectual evolution? Against Himmelfarb, others have argued for an essential continuity; the publication of the magnificent Toronto edition of the complete works over the past thirty-five years is said to have made this clear (O'Grady, 1991, p. 13). But this is still an issue for discussion; and related to it is an important debate about whether Mill, after his encounters with the Coleridgeans and de Tocqueville, remained a democrat (Burns, 1969; Zimmer, 1976; Francis & Morrow, 1994).

Third, how influential was Harriet Taylor Mill, and what was the nature and quality of that influence? Mill, as we have seen, himself insisted that her influence was paramount and all to the good. Others took a quite different view. Carlyle thought she was 'full of unwise intellect, asking and re-asking stupid questions', with her 'great dark eyes, that were flashing unutterable things while he was discoursin' the utterable concerning all sorts o' high topics' (Himmelfarb, 1974, p. 225). And according to Alexander Bain, Mill's friend, disciple and biographer, 'The more common way of representing Mrs Mill's ascendancy, is to say that she imbibed all his views, and gave them back in her own form, by which he was flattered and pleased' (Bain, 1882, p. 173). Hayek however proved from their correspondence that she did influence parts of his *Principles of Political Economy* (Hayek, 1951), and

Packe goes so far as to say that her influence was substantial on every major work Mill published after the *Political Economy*:

> In so far as Mill's influence, theoretic or applied, has been of advantage to the progress of the western world, or indeed of humanity at large, the credit should rest upon his wife at least as much as on himself (Packe, 1954, p. 371).

The contrary was argued by Pappe (Pappe, 1960; Robson, 1968, p. 53). This debate has acquired new urgency with the revival of the women's movement since the end of the 1960s. So, for example, Harriet Taylor Mill and her influence have been defended by Alice Rossi and Kate Soper, while Okin has agreed with Pappe (Rossi, 1970; Soper, 1983; Okin, 1979).

'Mill's writings in support of political, legal and social equality for women...read today like a series of truisms' (McCloskey, 1971, pp. 135–6). In these respects 'the world has gone completely as he would have wished' (Russell, 1969, p. 10). Such judgements seemed obvious in the 1960s: but they were always wrong. Their 'Western' bias is astonishing; over most of the globe Mill's aspirations for women are still unrealized. Even in the West his feminism does not command universal, wholehearted acceptance; the odd academic philosopher can still be found ready to suggest that women are naturally inferior to men, are adapted to a subordinate and domestic role and that *The Subjection of Women* is the 'ridiculous and discreditable' product of a self-important and under-sexed author (Stove, 1993, p. 12).

There is a far more important reason for challenging the 1960s verdict that *The Subjection of Women* is a set of truisms: in the subsequent revival of feminism, Mill's book has again become highly controversial. Of course modern feminists find words of praise for Mill – 'the first major philosopher since Plato to have argued that goodness was the same in a woman as in a man' (Okin, 1979, p. 220) but often the praise is faint. It is suggested that he was quite good for a man, but not altogether satisfactory, because he was a liberal, or allowed gender stereotypes back in, or accepted the bourgeois family, or expected women to conform to a masculine ideal of excellence – or simply because he was a man. Annas has argued that his essay was weak and contradictory, Mendus that his ideal of marriage was depressing, and Caine that his behaviour towards the emerging women's movement was patronizing and obstructive (Annas, 1977; Mendus, 1989; Caine, 1978). Others have been more positive (Tulloch, 1989; Shanley, 1991; Donner, 1993; Mendus, 1994); at the end of the twentieth century, this is a key debate about Mill.

As well as questions about the thought, there are questions about the man and his life. Was his parliamentary career a success or a failure? And why did he lose the radical constituency of Westminster, after an extension of the franchise should in theory have made it more safe? What kind of a man was he? The student of Mill cannot fail to notice an undercurrent of snide remarks in the literature; Mill was a good man, but.... Leslie Stephen, who wrote the DNB entry, set the pattern:

> His feelings, however, were, I take it, as tender as a woman's. They were wanting, not in keenness, but in the massiveness which implies more masculine fibre...The most eminent women, hitherto at least, are remarkable rather for docility than originality. Mill was especially remarkable, as I have said, for his power of assimilation. No more receptive pupil could ever be desired by a teacher. Like a woman, he took things – even philosophers – with excessive seriousness: and shows the complete want of humour often – unjustly perhaps – attributed to women (Stephen, 1912, p. 72).

A picture has developed of a chilly, bloodless man, over-intellectual, under-sexed, uxorious, priggish and humourless. One might explain this by remarking that people do not like those who preach at them, and Mill was certainly both moralistic and evangelical. Alternatively, one might think Mill was right in his complaint that the English are reluctant to credit those who claim to be motivated by anything other than self-interest.

More dramatically, Mill has been a victim of psychohistory, most notably at the hands of Bruce Mazlish (Mazlish, 1975; Glassman, 1985). His *Autobiography* encourages such attention, with its account of his extraordinary high-pressure education, his closeness to his father and the failure of the final version to mention his mother. According to Glassman, his upbringing was 'cruel and dehumanizing', 'few fathers ever have damaged a son so gravely', with the result that he lived an 'epically unhappy life'. Mill tells us that he began to come out of the mental crisis which began in 1826 when he read a passage in Marmontel's *Memoirs* in which the hero's father dies, and he, a mere boy, tells his family 'that he would be everything to them – would supply the place of all that they had lost' (*CW*, vol. I, p. 145). Mill was moved to tears, and greatly relieved; he could still feel after all. Amateur Freudians have seized on this to argue that Mill had an unconscious Oedipal desire to murder his father and marry his mother. Alternatively, it has been proposed that he had an inverse Oedipal complex, wishing to murder his mother and marry his father. I agree with Ryan's dismissal of the 'vulgarity and silliness' of all this: 'The one full-length attempt at a "psycho-biography" of James and John Stuart Mill produced so far was so inept that it was an embarrassment to read or review' (Ryan, 1991, p. 121). But, Freudian explanations apart, there *are* issues here: Was his education cruel and unusual? And did his unusually troubled and difficult emotional development have any effect on his philosophy?

The latest big issue in Mill scholarship grows out of new method-ologies in the history of ideas, which continue the 'hermeneutic' turn mentioned earlier. Poststructuralism has encouraged us to pay atten-tion to the languages or discourses, the traditions of thought or paradigms which shape texts. The classic study in this genre has been J.G.A. Pocock's work on the 'classical republican paradigm' (Pocock, 1975). This methodological fashion has prompted historians of ideas to pose the question as to which discursive contexts shaped Mill's thought? His *Autobiography* apparently gives a clear answer: the British and French Enlightenments, mediated especially through Benthamite philosophic radicalism and political economy; a dash of German Romanticism; and a great deal of modern French philosophical history and sociology, for example in the Saint-Simonians and Comte, Guizot and de Tocqueville.

There appears to be a puzzle here; Mill claims that the abstract and ahistorical mode of Benthamism was corrected for him by French thinkers who taught him to recognize historical diversity and relativity. They showed him that it was unacceptable to argue, in the abstract, that democracy is good: the proper question is what political system is appropriate to a particular place and time in history. But, as historians of ideas claim, this 'historical' approach was already central to the thought of the Scottish Enlightenment of the eighteenth century, expressed in books which Mill had read in his teens. So why did Mill situate himself in a French discourse rather than in a British one? Because, it has been said, he had an irrational dislike of England, and liked to cast himself in the role of an outsider; but, in reality, the discourse of British Whig historical sociology and politics determined the cast of his mind more than he admitted even to himself (Collini,

Winch & Burrow, 1983; Burrow, 1988). The most recent work in this *genre* has sought to relate Mill to a nineteenth-century speech-community of intellectuals and politicians, speaking to each other through the medium of the journals of comment and in the London clubs, whose discourse was structured around the ideas of altruism and character (Collini, 1991). This methodology offers the possibility of a profounder understanding of Mill's texts; but it is troubling that it conflicts so markedly with his own self-understanding, it has not gone unchallenged (Hamburger, 1989) and it will be questioned in the chapters which follow.

2

AUTOBIOGRAPHY AND NARRATIVES

Mill's *Autobiography* was published posthumously in 1873. The first six chapters had been drafted by 1854; they covered his life up to 1840 (*CW*, vol. I, pp. xxi–ii). His wife edited his early draft. The Mills thought the book important; it was to contain a condensed summary of their opinions, to be offered to the world after their deaths. They knew that some of those opinions would be unpopular, but were all the more determined to assert them; this was particularly the case with Mill's avowed religious agnosticism. The *Autobiography* was also to be a defence of their relationship, showing that it had been purely spiritual before the death of Harriet's husband John Taylor and their subsequent marriage. It justifies Mill's devotion to Harriet in terms of the transcendent qualities of her mind. The final chapter, 'General view of the remainder of my life' was written after 1869.

It is a remarkable book, one of the handful of great autobiographies, and a major contribution to European history. Though it tells a largely uneventful story about books and ideas, it is absorbing and moving, in spite of Carlyle's charge that it was 'the life of a logic-chopping engine, little more of human in it than if it had been done by a thing of mechanized iron', the 'autobiography of a steam-engine' (Himmelfarb, 1974, p. 188n). It is far from being a mere factual chronicle; the life has been shaped into a narrative with a dramatic structure, highlighting certain events and episodes. It has been suggested that the *Autobiography*, *because* it is an artistically shaped narrative, is unreliable as biographical history (Stillinger, 1991, p. 34). Such judgements must be taken with caution. All autobiography or self-understanding requires a measure of narrative selection and organizing, otherwise it would be shapeless and meaningless; a strong dramatic structuring, such as we find in Mill's *Autobiography*, may reveal aspects of the truth more vividly and forcefully. But as historians we have to be attentive to the *other* narratives that could have been told, the suppressed, ignored or forgotten narratives. Accordingly this chapter divides into two sections. First, it will explain the structure and essence of Mill's narrative, supplementing and illuminating the *Autobiography*'s account with reference to other writings. Second, it will point to places where the narrative is misleading or wrong and indicate what it ignores.

Mill's Narrative of his Life

Mill's *Autobiography* resembles the established genre of the *Bildungsroman*, the story of personal development. That is to say, it is centrally concerned not with outward events but with the inner life of its subject, and with that subject's growth to wholeness and maturity, with 'self-cultivation' as Mill refers to it. The genre is often associated with German romantic models, perhaps especially with the work of Goethe; Mill tells us that 'Goethe's device, "many-sidedness", was one which I would most willingly, at this period [the early 1830s], have taken for mine' (*CW*, vol. I, p. 171). But it was a well-established English genre too; we here observe Mill's persistent preference for the citation of European influences rather than British ones.

It is the story of how a one-sided youth became a many-sided man. To fill out this story it helps to read the *Autobiography* alongside the correspondence, debating speeches and essays. Mill begins with his remarkable education. In the final draft he tells us that his main aim is to acknowledge the debts which his intellectual and moral development owed to others, and the first two chapters are a tribute to his father. It is impossible to read them without being struck by how much Mill learned, and how young; his claim that it gave him a start of a quarter of a century over his contemporaries is plausible, but his assertion that he was below average in natural gifts will convince no-one (*CW*, vol. I, p. 33). Mill's claims follow from and are intended to lend credence to the psychological theory known as associationism, according to which abilities are not innate but produced by environment and education. It is noteworthy, and wholly characteristic, that Mill should say that with a similar education his achievements could be matched by any boy *or girl*. Another noteworthy matter is his emphatic rejection of Carlyle's accusation that Mill was a 'made' man, manufactured by his father, the passive product of another's will. Mill insists that 'Mine...was not an education of cram.' He was always encouraged by his father to discover things for himself (*CW*, vol. I, pp. 31–4).

Mill's tribute to his father as an educator is shadowed by criticism. He tells us that his education was purely intellectual; he never learned practical things, and was lamentably deficient in manual dexterity. His education was culturally impoverished; his father told him that 'people in general attached more value to verse than it deserved' (*CW*, vol. I, p. 19); he was not an admirer of Shakespeare, cared little for most English poetry and saw scarcely any merit in modern poetry. James Mill despised passionate emotions, thought that pleasure was greatly overrated and inculcated the classical Greek virtue of temperance, of self-restraint: 'He thought human life a poor thing at best, after the freshness of youth and of unsatisfied curiosity had gone by' (*CW*, vol. I, p. 49). But Mill's main criticism of his education is that it was based on fear. His father was stern and irritable, incapable of demonstrations of affection; he did not praise his son, for fear it would make him conceited. Mill concedes that a worthwhile education cannot all be easy and enjoyable; discipline is essential, and an element of fear indispensable. But when it predominates, it shrivels the spontaneous affections (*CW*, vol. I, p. 55).

A significant commentary on his education is provided by his year in France when he was fourteen. He 'breathed for a whole year the free and genial atmosphere of Continental life' (*CW*, vol. I, p. 59). 'Free' seems obvious enough; here is a veiled criticism of the constraints and oppression of his father's educational régime. But 'genial'? It was only later, he tells us, that the contrast between France and England came into clear focus for him. In France he found 'elevated sentiments', a 'habitual exercise of the feelings', 'frank sociability and amiability'. In England by contrast there is 'sneering depreciation' of 'high feelings', cynicism about principles, selfishness, and a tendency to treat everybody as 'either an enemy or a bore' (*CW*, vol. I, pp. 59, 61). This is caricature, as comparisons of 'national character' always are; but it is a theme which runs through Mill's maturity. He always felt at home in France.

He returned to England, read Bentham, and thereby acquired a philosophy and purpose in life (*CW*, vol. I, p. 69). With 'youthful fanaticism' and a 'sectarian spirit', he set about fulfilling it, writing for the *Westminster Review*, collecting around him a group of young men so as to form a school of 'philosophic radicals' in imitation of the French *philosophes* of the eighteenth century, campaigning for population control, representative government and free speech, and in the process becoming a 'mere reasoning machine' (*CW*, vol. I, p. 111).

With great artistry, Mill has built up to the dramatic climax, which comes at the centre of the book: the mental crisis in his twentieth year.

> I was in a dull state of nerves ... In this frame of mind it occurred to me to put the question directly to myself, 'Suppose that all your objects in life were realized; that all the changes in institutions and opinions which you are looking forward to, could be completely effected at this very instant: would this be a great joy and happiness to you?' and an irrepressible self-consciousness distinctly answered, 'No!' At this my heart sank within me: the whole foundation on which my life was constructed fell down. ... I seemed to have nothing left to live for (*CW*, vol. I, pp. 138–9).

Most twentieth-century doctors would diagnose a depressive illness; Freudians would suspect a complex. Mill chooses to explain his crisis as a philosophical one. He uses it to illuminate the problems of the philosophy of mind, the theory of Association in which he had been brought up. At the same time, he employs it to demonstrate the well-nigh catastrophic failure of the education he had received at his father's hands. For example, in the first place, Associationism takes it as axiomatic that individuals act only when motivated by desires and aversions, and that the fundamental desire is for pleasure. But his father had taught him that pleasure was a poor thing, and in any case his education had developed his reason without teaching him to enjoy himself.

Second, Associationism goes hand-in-hand with the 'doctrine of necessity', or as we would call it today, the theory of determinism. That is to say, it explains all our actions as caused. What I do is caused by my strongest desire or group of desires immediately prior to acting; my desires themselves are caused by the ideas and experiences which immediately precede them, which are caused by what went before, and so on, back down an unending causal chain. Each state of affairs is determined by the state of affairs before it, which means that what happens *has* to happen. It follows that choice, if by choice I mean that I could have done other than I did, is an illusion. To Mill, as to many others before and since, this was a deeply depressing doctrine:

> I felt as if I was scientifically proved to be the helpless slave of antecedent circumstances; as if my character and that of all others had

been formed for us by agencies beyond our control, and was wholly out of our own power (*CW*, vol. I, pp. 175–6).

Associationism theorizes the self as the passive product of its experiences, most of which take the form of impressions entering the mind through the five senses. To illustrate it with Bradley's scornful simile, sense-impressions collect in the mind as in a bag (Bradley, 1927, p. 35). Now, unlike ordinary bagfuls, this one is not entirely without structure; for example, ideas which resemble each other will group together, and the mind associates some ideas with pleasure, others with pain. But still, the self is nothing other than this collection, this bag of ideas coming largely from outside. The character of the individual is caused in this way by external circumstances. Mill was not happy with this doctrine.

Third, Associationism failed to support Mill's moral and political philosophy. His utilitarian purpose in life was to promote the greatest happiness of the greatest number, i.e. to be altruistic. This would only be possible, and would only satisfy him, if he actually desired the happiness of others, if he could sympathize with their pleasures and pains. But Associationism, influenced by the philosopher of self-interest Thomas Hobbes (1588–1679) proposed that the original desire of each individual was a selfish desire for his own happiness. The theory argued that altruistic desires developed, by a process of association, out of that original selfish desire. The Associationist philosopher Hartley (1705–57) gives an example; when we are children, if a parent is ill, we suffer pains and privations. The usual treats and outings cannot be provided, we cannot play in our usual boisterous manner. We associate our own unhappiness with the sufferings of others, and because these impressions are formed early and repeated, this association happens spontaneously, without reflection. The sight of others in pain immediately makes us miserable, dredging up childhood feelings from the deep recesses of the mind: we have acquired the faculty of sympathy. Mill had accepted this theory; but now he realized that it was no use. For it proposes that sympathy is based on a mistake: the habit of mistaking, by unconscious processes of association, the pleasures and pains of others for our own. But Mill had been trained in analysis, and analysis had the power to expose the mistake and dissolve the association. Analysis revealed that there was no reason to desire the good of others, and that such a desire was not an original part of the constitution of the mind.

I was thus, as I said to myself, left stranded at the commencement of my voyage, with a well equipped ship and rudder, but no sail; without any real desire for the ends which I had been so carefully fitted out to work for: no delight in virtue or the general good, but also just as little in anything else (*CW*, vol. I, p. 143).

As we saw earlier, he began to recover when, weeping over Marmontel's *Memoirs*, he discovered that his sympathies were not dead. He also found pleasure in Wordsworth's poetry. As a result he realized that his education had been but a half-education, for it had developed his intellect without cultivating his feelings. From now on, he stressed 'the internal culture of the individual'. His concern for poetry and culture points to his sense of the philistinism of Benthamite radicalism. He wanted a richer, more varied mental diet than he thought his father had given him. It also reveals him correcting, as he saw it, the deficiencies of the Enlightenment by invoking the philosophy of Romanticism. For at the heart of Romanticism is a quite different account of the self. Whereas Associationism refers the self to external circumstances and renders it passive, a collection of sense-impressions in a bag, Romanticism turns inward, proposing an active self with an inherent tendency to growth and development, a self-creating self, a self which pours out and expresses its inner life, a self which is not a collection but a whole. Mill translates this vision, the vision of Goethe, Coleridge or Shelley, into his own prosaic terms. For instance, in this way he resolved, to his own satisfaction, the 'doctrine of necessity' – the problem of determinism. My self is a product of external circumstances; but if I desire to change, then I can take action to shape those circumstances; for example, I can mix with the kind of people who will have a good effect upon me. By such means I have the power to form my own character, to take charge of my own destiny (*CW*, vol. I, p. 177).

This is to adopt a strategy which is commonly used to defend determinism against its critics: Mill argues that the causal determination of human behaviour, properly understood, is perfectly compatible with our commonsense belief in our own freedom. The two only seem incompatible when determinism is *misunderstood*, when it is taken to imply more than it really does imply. The problem stems from that word *necessity*. We must not fall into the trap of supposing it implies that our will is powerless; that what will be, will be, whether we will it or not. As Mill insists, the state of the agent's will, what she actually desires, is one of the antecedent circumstances which determine what she does; the doctrine of necessity does not suppose that we are determined to act *against* our wills. The will of the agent, what she wants in any particular situation, is itself in part determined by her character. But, as we have seen, this does not imply that we are the helpless slaves of whatever character we happen to have; if we wish it, we can take steps to *change* our characters.

If we wish it – Mill recognizes that the wish to change one's character is itself caused by some external influence. Does this mean that in the last resort we are not free? Yes, Mill replies – but he insists that this does not matter. There is all the difference in the world between the false statement that we do not have the power to change our characters, and the true statement that we will not use that power unless something causes us to use it. Mill believes that the former statement, if true, would deny us the freedom we feel we have and which we want to have: the latter statement is perfectly compatible with our sense of our freedom.

This argument modifies and restates Associationism without abandoning it. Many critics have thought that Mill's incorporation of Romanticism into his philosophical heritage was incomplete. Dissatisfied with a pure diet of reason and analysis, he invokes feeling and poetry in compensation. But this fails to challenge the superficial rationalism of his mentors. Reason and feeling, analysis and poetry exist for Mill in separate compartments, unaffected by each other. He never arrives, as Coleridge did, at a different conception of *experience*, one which repudiates the separation of reason and feeling, recognizing that 'reason' is never pure, detached and perfectly objective (Williams, 1963, pp. 81–3).

Mill's first great statement of the need to correct the Enlightenment by invoking Romanticism was not the draft of his *Autobiography* written in the early 1850s; it came in his essay on Bentham of 1838. It is a devastating exposure of the inadequacy of the Benthamite account of the self; an exercise, it has been said, in intellectual parricide. In order to be qualified as a moral and political philosopher, Mill argues, it is necessary to know a great deal about human nature and human life. But Bentham's range of experience was extraordinarily narrow:

> He was a boy to the last. Self-consciousness, that daemon of the men of genius of our time, from Wordsworth to Byron, from Goethe to Chateaubriand … never was awakened in him. … His general conception of human nature and life, furnished him with an unusually slender stock of premises (*CW*, vol. X, pp. 92–3).

Mill invokes the Romantics to correct the one-sidedness of Bentham and what he especially mentions is Romantic self-consciousness and self-knowledge. The Romantics have a fuller and a deeper knowledge of human nature than Bentham ever did.

So what does Mill think is missing from Bentham's conception of human nature? 'Man is never recognized by him as a being capable of pursuing spiritual perfection as an end' (*CW*, vol. X, p. 95). This is a substantial departure from Benthamite Utilitarianism. Bentham imagines humans as beings who desire pleasure, and this encourages a conception of human beings as consumers. Mill would have us recognize that human beings are much more than that; the individual is also active, a creator, capable of creating herself in accordance with a standard of personal excellence which she has herself chosen. Furthermore, in search of that complex entity, happiness, humans pursue other ends of which Bentham was scarcely aware: honour, dignity, beauty, order, power and action. Bentham also thinks that human conduct is largely controlled in a mechanical way by external sanctions – the fear of punishment by God or the state, the fear of the disapproval of our fellows. Mill by contrast looks within, to the internal policeman which each person carries around inside, to the conscience. Mill therefore gives a much richer description of the inner life of the individual than does Bentham.

The story of Mill the apostate from Benthamism was being told by Mill in its strongest form when he was a young man in the 1830s; no doubt it was part of an attempt to define himself as his own person. By the time he wrote the *Autobiography*, he thought that to some extent he had established his distinctiveness by caricaturing his mentors. So for example he tells us that he had undervalued the eighteenth century, but never joined in the reaction against it; if he had entered into a full and frank explanation with his father, the latter would have considered his son a deserter, but his distance from his father had more to do with mood and style than with matters of substance: 'I am ... inclined to think that my father was not so much opposed as he seemed, to the modes of thought in which I believed myself to differ from him' (*CW*, vol. I, pp. 169, 189, 209, 211). I think this is fair commentary on matters of political policy; in the 1830s Mill exaggerated the extent to which he moved from philosophic radicalism towards philosophic toryism, as I argue below. Nevertheless, the *Autobiography* tells us that he *abandoned* the political philosophy of his youth (*CW*, vol. I, p. 169), and the essay on Bentham, which is consistent with his later ethical writings, reveals the distance he travelled from his mentors on fundamental moral issues.

The early debating speeches, when Mill crossed swords with other young men who were *not* 'philosophic radicals', and the youthful journalism and correspondence, throw further light on his odyssey. At first the reader gets a picture of a callow youth, hard, dogmatic and abrasive. There is more than a touch of philistinism – for example, poets and dramatists are virtually useless (*CW*, vol. XXVI, p. 352). A neo-Hobbesian doctrine of near-universal selfishness, which plays a pivotal role in his father's *Essay on Government*, is very much in evidence. It is utopian to suppose that people will sacrifice self-interest for the public good (*CW*, vol. XXII, p. 40); all men who have power will infallibly abuse it (*CW*, vol. XXII, p. 63). The opinions of ninety-nine out of one hundred men are of no value when their interests are involved; priests discourage population control because they make money out of marriages, baptisms and funerals (*CW*, vol. VI, pp. 80, 85). All aristocrats and lawyers are corrupt and selfish. It is clear that Mill was painting himself into a corner. Not only is his doctrine crudely false; it also leads him into contradictions. Mill is *attacking* aristocrats, lawyers and priests for their selfishness: but if selfishness is virtually universal and ineluctable, then how can anybody be blamed for it? Moreover, Mill's style of argument imputes selfishness to his conservative opponents, but implies that he and his radical allies are the exceptional one per cent who are principled and altruistic. Sometimes this implausible contrast becomes explicit, as when he attacks co-operative socialist followers of Robert Owen (1771–1858) for ignoring self-love, and then goes on to claim that a pure flame of benevolence burns in the bosoms of political economists like himself (*CW*, vol. XXVI, pp. 324–5). In due course this theoretical problem became a problem of personal relationships for Mill. The argument became one about *character*, with much trading of insults. His speeches are often rude about his opponents, attributing their ideas to base and selfish motives and dull stupidity. His *Times* obituary by Hayward proves that he caused deep and lasting offence. Perhaps the dislike of Hayward did not bother him; but in due course he offended John Sterling, a man whose friendship he desired. His speech on the French *philosophe* Montesquieu (1689–1755) of 3 April 1829 reveals him in anguish; Sterling has evidently abused Mill as Mill had formerly abused the Tories (*CW*, vol. XXVI, pp. 443–8). Mill resigned from the debating society, writing to Sterling with overtures of friendship (*CW*, vol. XII, pp. 29–30).

Mill had come to realize that the Benthamite theory of moral motivation needed rethinking (Hampsher-Monk, 1992, p. 363). A few years
later he would write that, although Bentham did not think that humans
were wholly selfish, his language gave that impression and therefore
his writings caused moral harm (*CW*, vol. X, pp. 12–15). It seems likely
that he had also learnt that the *style* of argument of Bentham and James
Mill was seriously defective, shrill, aggressive and unconciliatory. And
he had come to think that their confident assertion of timeless human
traits (for example, selfishness) as first principles of political philosophy
paid too little attention to historical circumstances and diversity.

If we return from these other writings to the *Autobiography* its essential dialectical structure now stands revealed. The thesis is philosophic
radicalism, characterized by science, logic, analysis and criticism, which
fails because of its inadequacies and contradictions. The antithesis is
Romanticism (though Mill does not use this term), characterized by
poetry, feeling, the culture of the self and other ideas which we shall
consider presently. The synthesis is a combination of the two. Mill's life
is narrated as an evolution towards that synthesis; but he suggests he
never achieved it. Evidently he thought that the poetic and visionary
capacities of a Coleridge, Wordsworth or Carlyle were lacking or imperfectly developed in himself; his strengths lay in logic, criticism and sustained reasoning. The synthesis is embodied in Harriet Taylor, who
was a fully rounded, complete human being (*CW*, vol. XII, pp. 113,
118; vol. XV, p. 610). It is as if he achieved wholeness vicariously, by
identifying with her.

The *Autobiography*, therefore, narrates Mill's odyssey from the influence of his father to the influence of his wife. His original intention for
the organization of the book would have made this plain. There were to
have been two parts, and part two began with the chapter which introduced Harriet Taylor, 'Commencement of the Most Valuable Friendship
of My Life. My Father's Death.' But there were other influences, presented by Mill as of less importance, which must now be considered.

'The influences of European, that is to say, continental, thought, and
especially those of the reaction of the nineteenth century against the
eighteenth, were now streaming in upon me' (*CW*, vol. I, p. 169). As Mill
saw it, the eighteenth century lacked a proper philosophy of history;
he endorsed the view, which later became something of a commonplace, that the Enlightenment was unhistorical. Continental thought of
the nineteenth century provided a corrective. One of the two main elements he borrowed was a plot or script for the grand sweep of human

(or at least of Occidental) history. Mill thought of this as a process in which human and rational characteristics steadily prevailed over brutal ones, in which mind gained predominance over matter. When he became acquainted with the thought of the Saint-Simonians in the late 1820s, he drew on their ideas in order to elaborate his narrative. This elaboration is the main theme of his essay 'The Spirit of the Age' of 1831.

There Mill distinguishes between 'natural' and 'transitional' periods. Natural periods are stable; rule is exercised by those fittest to rule. The masses take their opinions from their rulers, hence there is a consensus which ensures social stability. Mill proposes that European history moves through three great natural periods. First came the age of the classical republics of Greece and Rome, when the citizens chose the best men to rule and lead the people in battle. Second came the medieval world of Catholic Christianity, of monarchs and landed aristocrats. This was rule by the best, not in the sense that the best were chosen, rather that the hereditary rulers *became* the best by virtue of their unique training for warfare and rule. Mill breaks with harder-nosed spokesmen of the radical Enlightenment, who thought of the Middle Ages as a period of stagnation and superstition, by conceding that the dominance of Catholic church and hereditary aristocracy was the best system *for that time*, thereby to some extent aligning himself with the romantic enthusiasm for things medieval. The third great period is soon to come; society will be led by the best minds, scientifically trained and chosen for their excellence.

Transitional periods are ones in which those who rule are not the best; they are challenged by an outgroup of more able and cultivated minds. Mill thought that his own was such a period and that he was one of those outsiders, pitted against a decaying and delegitimated hereditary aristocracy. In transitional periods, when authority is questioned, there is an unstable anarchy of opinion, scepticism and cynicism: such, Mill thought, was the unhappy predicament of his own time. In his later *Autobiography*, instead of 'natural' and 'transitional' epochs, he writes of 'organic' and 'critical' ones; organic ones are simply those in which there is a consensus which humankind eventually outgrows, critical ones are ages of criticism and negation when that consensus is destroyed (*CW*, vol. I, p. 171). This rewording subtly modifies the evaluations; 'organic' is less of a plus-word than 'natural', 'critical' carries positive connotations which 'transitional' does not.

A further ingredient was added to this philosophy of history when Mill read Comte's *Cours de Philosophie Positive* from 1837. He took the idea that each science – physics, biology, ethics, politics etc. – moves through three stages towards perfection: the religious, the metaphysical and finally the positive or scientific stage. Mill thought that the physical sciences had already reached the final stage and that the human or moral sciences were in the process of attaining it, led by psychology and economics (neither of which, incidentally, were recognized as sciences by Comte himself). This informed Mill's conception of the 'natural' stage of society which was about to come: in best Saint-Simonian or Comtian fashion, Mill thought the hereditary aristocracy would give way to a leading élite of scientific experts.

A few comments are needed about the philosophy of history to be found in 'The Spirit of the Age'. In the first place, it is more idealist than materialist, closer in spirit to Hegel than to Marx. In the foreground stand changes in ideas and institutions, and institutions mostly means *political* institutions. Mill mentions non-ideal factors in his account of historical dynamics – for example, increased facility of communication because of large cities, faster transport and the printing press – but there is no theory of change being driven primarily by economic transformations. In his second essay on de Tocqueville, he explicitly repudiates economic determinism: 'Ideas are not always the mere signs and effects of social circumstances, they are themselves a power in history'. In the same essay he repudiates any notion that progress is inevitable, thereby marking a distinction between his theory and that of 'historicists' such as Marx or Hegel who believed that history was largely scripted in advance (*CW*, vol. XVIII, pp. 197–8).

Second, this philosophy of history is closer to the Enlightenment than Mill appears to think; it narrates progress, laying stress upon the advance of knowledge and the growth of civility, refinement and security in a way which would not have surprised such eighteenth-century philosophers as Hume, Turgot or Condorcet. Third, it is part of Mill's strategy for making sense of his own life and development. He is surely thinking of his mental crisis as a phenomenon at the micro level intimately bound up with the strains and uncertainties of a society in 'critical' phase at the macro level. His return to mental health after a long struggle, as he enriched his conceptions and thought through his intellectual problems, anticipates the 'organic' phase which is to come. Finally, this philosophy of history engendered a theoretical tension. From his father and Bentham he inherited a passion for freedom of thought and discussion. Yet the theory of natural and transitional stages suggested that difference of opinion was primarily characteristic of an

age of transition; and the positivist conception of scientific advance
proposed that as time went on disputed questions would be cleared up.
In that case, what would be the point of rival opinions and freedom of
thought? After all, who questions the multiplication tables or the laws
of gravity?

Mill's historical thinking drew inspiration from another quarter. His
most brilliant, influential and misleading account of 'the revolt of the
human mind against the philosophy of the eighteenth century' (*CW*,
vol. X, p. 125) is contained in his essay 'Coleridge' of 1840, the companion to his essay on Bentham. He returns to his preoccupation with
the culture of the self, which he thought that philosophic radicalism
neglected. The trouble with the Enlightenment was that its thrust was
almost entirely critical and destructive. The *philosophes* thought, he
explains, that human nature in itself is good; evil stems from false
beliefs and bad institutions. Tear these down, virtue will flourish and all
will be happy. But if, as Associationism contends, the original and fundamental motivations are selfish, why should we expect humans to live
in harmony once all the restraints have been removed? Mill found a
solution to this problem in the 'philosophy of culture' of the 'Germano-
Coleridgean school'. (Mill specifically refers to a number of late eighteenth and early nineteenth-century sources: 'the Goethian period of
German literature', Herder, and the French historians who followed
and interpreted the Germans, such as Michelet and Guizot) (*CW*, vol. X,
pp. 139–41).

The Germano-Coleridgeans recognized, he thought, that the whole
system of a society's 'opinions and observances' played a part in securing
peace and social co-operation. Three things were principally required:
first, a system of education, formal and informal, which would act as
a restraining discipline, bringing to bear on the individual such influences as religion, poetry and law; second, a feeling of common allegiance or loyalty to persons or fundamental institutions; third, 'a strong
and active principle of nationality', a sense of community and common
interest. Given these things, natural selfishness can be restrained, and
peaceful co-existence secured. The Germano-Coleridgeans knew this,
and so they approached the past with an attitude of reverence. Each
peaceful age, each stable society, must be understood sympathetically
in its own terms, as a system which works for reasons which are not
immediately apparent. Benthamite universal laws and abstractions
are no match for Germano-Coleridgean complexity and historical
understanding: 'They thus produced, not a piece of party advocacy,

but…a contribution, the largest yet made by any class of thinkers, towards the philosophy of human culture' (*CW*, vol. X, p. 139).

From them Mill had learnt 'that all questions of political institutions are relative, not absolute, and that different stages of human progress not only *will* have, but *ought* to have, different institutions' (*CW*, vol. I, p. 169). Therefore he was bound to conclude that the advocacy of democracy by the philosophic radicals was too simplistic and blind to the difficulties: 'I ceased to consider representative democracy as an absolute principle, and regarded it as a question of time, place, and circumstance' (*CW*, vol. I, p. 177). His position on this issue at this time can be found in his essay 'Civilization' of 1836, and his two essays on 'Tocqueville on Democracy in America' of 1835 and 1840. (Alexis de Tocqueville, 1805–59, was a French politician and historian whose book on America appeared 1835–40.) Mill distinguishes between democratic institutions and democratic society; the latter is characterized by 'equality of conditions', and both are the antithesis of aristocracy. Mill does not doubt the desirability of democratic institutions, though his version of them would not please all democrats, as we shall see later.

The problem is democratic society. Because its principle is equality, it poses a threat to excellence and encourages mediocrity. Individuality is constantly at risk, in danger of being swallowed up by the mass. The commercial middle classes who dominate a democratic society do not love diversity and dissenting thought, and they exercise pressure for conformity through the medium of public opinion as expressed in the press. In terms borrowed from Coleridge, Mill laments the possibility that civilization will develop at the expense of higher cultivation (*CW*, vol. XVIII, p. 143), and that a society where the principle of commerce reigns unchallenged will be characterized by Chinese stationariness (*CW*, vol. XVIII, p. 197). Progress depends upon a principle of antagonism, which in a commercial society must be found in three elements: an agricultural class, a leisured class, and a learned class (*CW*, vol. XVIII, p. 198). This echoes, but in a less conservative manner, Coleridge's demand for a counterbalance to the spirit of trade. Mill's learned class resembles Coleridge's 'clerisy', a cohort of priests, academics and teachers supported by public endowment – though Mill, unlike Coleridge, has no time for a clerisy dominated by an established church or indeed by any church; that would be hostile to freedom of thought (*CW*, vol. XVIII, pp. 143–4). And Mill's agricultural class and leisured class do not correspond to the landed aristocracy which Coleridge requires as a counterpoise to the mercantile element.

Mill's agriculturists are farmers and peasants, a sector of society which he always respected.

In considering the further influences which flowed in upon Mill after his mental crisis, we have found him keeping bad company for a radical – Coleridge, Wordsworth, Carlyle, de Tocqueville, the French liberal-conservative politician and historian Guizot. This has led to the interpretation, quite widespread but most strongly argued by Himmelfarb, that Mill at this time passed through a 'conservative' phase. It has been said that his sense of the need for authority and leadership was so strong at this time as to contradict his earlier and later enthusiasms for democracy and liberty. There are passages in the *Autobiography* which appear to support this interpretation. Looking back, Mill opined that his critique of Bentham had been too severe, and his praise of Coleridge too generous (*CW*, vol. I, pp. 225, 227); in the third period of his mental development, when he advanced hand-in-hand with Harriet Taylor, he turned back from the excess of his reaction against Benthamism (*CW*, vol. I, p. 237). Some of his radical allies thought at the time that he had betrayed them; for example Mrs Grote complained about the direction taken by Mill's *London and Westminster Review:*

> Whether by getting hooks baited with carrion, he attracts other sorts of fish than those *we* angle for, and thus render it a better investment, I really am not in a condition to judge … For my part I only wonder how the people continue to keep improving, under the purveyance of the stuff and nonsense they are subjected to (Bain, 1882, p. 57n).

But Mill also writes that even when he rejected his father's *Essay on Government*, concluding that representative democracy was *not* suitable to all times and places, he continued to think that democracy was what Europe, and especially England, needed (*CW*, vol. I, pp. 169, 177). An open-minded reading of the great essays of the 1830s alongside the correspondence and lesser journalism confirms this, making it clear that the so-called conservative John Stuart Mill is an over-simplification, based on a selective and insensitive reading of the sources. In all of the essays, Mill is an implacable foe of hereditary aristocracy, 'the most useless, selfish, and unfeeling drones in human shape who live and kill game on the surface of the earth' (*CW*, vol. VI, p. 277), with their landed monopoly and enclosure of the commons, their corn laws and corrupt manipulation of the law and the tax system. Others had read de Tocqueville's *Democracy in America* as an attack on democracy: Mill insists that the book is a powerful defence of democratic institutions and he welcomes it as such. The essay 'Civilization' is a jeremiad, lamenting the effects of mass society, but it contains a ferocious attack on the established church, and on the universities of Oxford and Cambridge.

It is undoubtedly true that these essays are élitist, or more accurately meritocratic, and that, especially in 'The Spirit of the Age', Mill laments the absence of consensus in morals and politics and looks forward to a time when the uninstructed will have respect for the learned. Mill was prepared for this kind of élitism by his boyhood immersion in the writings of Plato, who advocated rule by 'philosopher-kings'. Another influence to put alongside Saint-Simonianism, Comte and Coleridge is that of his friend and mentor John Austin. Like Mill, Austin thought that we identify right and wrong actions, not by some immediate intuition which all possess, but by consulting the evidence and calculating which actions will promote the greatest happiness. Such calculations may require extensive and profound knowledge, for example of psychology or economics; hence the need for expert guidance (Friedman, 1969, pp. 389–95).

There may be a *tension* here between authority and freedom of thought; but there is not, as Cowling for example has implied, a *contradiction*. Mill thought that social consensus around truths established by the learned was desirable, but he never proposed to *enforce* mental conformity. His clearest repudiation of the tyranny of the expert is in *Auguste Comte and Positivism* of 1865 (Comte really did want to enforce the 'truth' and burn erroneous books) but similar opinions can be found from the time of 'The Spirit of the Age'. In November 1829 he wrote to d'Eichthal that a spiritual power, and deference and submission to authority, were needed but they should not be organized (*CW*, vol. XII, p. 40). And in his essay 'On Genius' of 1832 we find him insisting that no-one should trust an authority to dictate his duties (*CW*, vol. I, p. 338). Again, like Austin he believed that authority had to validate and revalidate itself in free discussion. In some ultimate sense Mill was not a pluralist (as Isaiah Berlin has interpreted him), for he believed that the truth was single; but he thought that consensus was a long way off, and it became more remote as he grew older (Knights, 1978, p. 169). If we distinguish between 'organic intellectuals' who teach the doctrines and values around which a society coheres, and an 'intelligentsia' which adopts a critical stance to the established order (Kent, 1978, p. 4), then we can say that in the 1830s Mill was impressed

by the need for organic intellectuals, or as he and Coleridge would
term it, a clerisy. But his own stance, throughout his life, was that of a
member of the intelligentsia.

It appears that Mill turned to Wordsworth, Coleridge and Carlyle not
for conservatism but to reinforce radicalism. What he praised them for
was not their attempt to preserve the past, but rather for encouraging
established institutions such as church and aristocracy to live up to
their ideals (*CW*, vol. I, p. 510). This was partly a rhetorical and political strategy; Mill was mischievously presenting enemies of radicalism as
critics of the established order. He continued to do this; in 1866 we
find him implying in parliament that Coleridge favoured taking land
from landlords and giving it to the people (*CW*, vol. XXVIII, p. 82).
But he also hoped to find new allies, to build a broader radicalism.
And this was not unreasonable; among the disciples of Coleridge was
Mill's friend F.D. Maurice, later a Christian socialist. There is a well-
known passage in a letter of 1831 to Mill's best friend of the time, the
Coleridgean John Sterling: 'Hence all my differences with [Wordsworth],
or with any other philosophic Tory, would be differences of matter-
of-fact or detail, while my differences with the radicals & utilitarians are
differences of principle' (*CW*, vol. XII, p. 81). One should not be misled by this. Mill and Sterling were united in their enthusiasm for the
French revolution of 1830 (in Mill's case this was a romantic enthusiasm for revolutionary working men worthy of Marx himself – *CW*,
vol. XII, pp. 55–7, 60, 62) and Sterling had recently been involved in
trying to finance a rebellion against the Spanish government. In the
1831 letter, Mill writes:

> If there were but a few dozens of persons safe…to be mission-
> aries of the great truths in which alone there is any well-being for
> mankind…I should not care though a revolution were to extermi-
> nate every person in Great Britain & Ireland who has £500 a year
> (*CW*, vol. XII, p. 84).

In 1834 Mill wrote that if the government took steps to repress trade
unions, then every man who could afford it should provide himself with
a musket (*CW*, vol. VI, p. 208); in 1842 he informed Comte that he
belonged to the moderate revolutionary party (*CW*, vol. XIII, p. 503)
and in 1847 he told Austin that England needed a revolution (*CW*,
vol. XII, p. 713). In keeping with this view of himself as a moderate
revolutionary, Mill persistently identified with the Girondins, who were

ousted by the more extreme Jacobins during the French Revolution of
1789 (*CW*, vol. XII, p. 165). The French revolution of 1848 aroused
his enthusiasm and he thought that the central current of European
history was to be found in France's revolutionary transformations (*CW*,
vol. XX, p. 230). Mill was never a conservative; he appears most
like one in some of his essays of 1840 when, under the influence of
de Tocqueville, his doubts about democracy were at their height. These
doubts will be discussed in a later chapter. In the last decade of his
life he moved to the left; that this has been insufficiently appreciated
is due to the fact that he wrote and published no major new work on
politics during that decade.

I have already noted Harriet Taylor Mill's place in Mill's *Autobiography*:
a little more needs to be said about it. Mill insisted that his greatest
intellectual debts were to her and we have seen how, in his view, a kind
of mental wholeness was attained in their union. But what specifically
did he think he learnt from her?

> There was a moment in my mental progress when I might easily have
> fallen into a tendency towards over-government, both social and
> political; as there was a moment when, by reaction from a contrary
> excess, I might have become a less thorough radical and democrat
> than I am (*CW*, vol. I, p. 259).

Harriet corrected both of these tendencies; in other words she confirmed
him in his commitments to radicalism, democracy and individual liberty
(*CW*, vol. I, p. 259). Mill insists that not only during the years of their
married life, but also during the years of their close friendship, his
published writings were as much her work as his, and that during the
greater part of his literary life he was her interpreter. But he affirms
that the first of his books in which her share was conspicuous was the
Principles of Political Economy (*CW*, vol. I, pp. 251, 255). In other words,
she played no part in the *System of Logic*, and presumably none in the
essays of the 1830s.

Her contribution to the *Political Economy*, on Mill's account, was crucial. For example, he was responsible for the purely technical part, but
she dictated much of the socialistic chapter on 'The Probable Future of
the Labouring Classes' which was added to the second edition. The
essay *On Liberty* was 'more directly and literally our joint production
than anything else which bears my name' (*CW*, vol. I, p. 257). *The
Subjection of Women* contained ideas contributed by his stepdaughter,

Helen Taylor, and even passages of her writing. But 'all that is most striking and profound belongs to my wife' (*CW*, vol. I, p. 265). The writing however was Mill's own work and Harriet did not live long enough to revise and improve it; he also declares that his commitment to sexual equality antedated his acquaintance with her (*CW*, vol. I, p. 253n). The essay on *Utilitarianism* was based on papers he had written during the last years of his married life, and the *Considerations on Representative Government* in 1860 or 1861. He makes no specific claim that his wife had anything to do with either, and this is in marked contrast to his statements about the *Political Economy*, *On Liberty* and *The Subjection of Women*.

In conclusion Mill narrates his life in such a way as to imbue it with complex meaning, inscribing it within a wider history. It is described as a journey from the chilly house of his father to the radiant home of his wife. This journey is also a process of *Bildung*, of self-development both emotional and intellectual. It is the story of how a man, with pain and travail of soul, created his own character. It has a Saint-Simonian pattern, from narrow certainty through doubt to an enriched certainty. It gains added significance by being described as going hand-in-hand with, and helping along, the evolution of European thought and culture. Mill's revolt against Benthamism is not narrated as a mere private affair; it purports to symbolize and give voice to the protest of a whole generation against the aridities of the Enlightenment. If we buy Mill's story, then we accept him as a cultural leader, a bellwether, one who lived and experienced the travails of the European soul as it took the next step foward; a representative man who articulated the issues of the age with peculiar insight and incisiveness.

Is Mill's Narrative True?

It has been suggested that Mill exaggerated the harshness of his childhood for rhetorical purposes, so as to make all the more dramatic the contrast between his earlier self, unpoetic and deprived of affection, and his later self, cultivated and beloved by Harriet (Stillinger, 1991). The reminiscences of others, and scraps of evidence within the *Autobiography* itself, support the view that there was the closest companionship between father and son, that Mill was not repressed and that there were more amusements than Mill's account of grinding intellectual labour suggests. But a letter by Francis Place tells of excessive severity and punishments, of cuffs and deprivation of dinner, and of long hours of work. In fact, the final version of the *Autobiography* toned down the strictures on James Mill. In an earlier draft we read 'I thus grew up in the absence of love and in the presence of fear: and many and indelible are the effects of this bringing-up, in the stunting of my moral growth' (*CW*, vol. I, p. 612). But Mill is surely unfair to blame his father for making him unpoetic; the list of poets that James Mill liked or gave his son to read includes Spenser, Milton, Dryden, Pope, Thomson, Goldsmith, Gray, Burns, Cowper, Beattie, Campbell and Scott.

A shadow of doubt also falls over his allegation that he grew up in a non-religious environment: 'I was brought up from the first without any religious belief... I am thus one of the very few examples, in this country, of one who has, not thrown off religious belief, but never had it' (*CW*, vol. I, pp. 41, 45). Mill's correspondence with Comte confirms a deep and passionate hostility to organized Christianity and its doctrine. But one of his earliest letters written when he was eight years old tells of going to church (*CW*, vol. XII, p. 5), and quotations and half-quotations in his writings throughout his life testify to a knowledge of the Bible such as few possess today.

A more significant issue is the soundness of his account of that central episode, the mental crisis of 1826–7. Mill's narrative, written a quarter of a century after the event, is the sole evidence for it; the chronology he provides is demonstrably suspect and it seems likely that he reinterpreted the experience in the light of the later evolution of his ideas (Cumming, 1964, pp. 235–56). If one sets aside neo-Freudian fantasies, other explanations than Mill's own are possible. Both Bain and Leslie Stephen bluntly put it down to overwork. Janice Carlisle has argued with some plausibility that it was a depression brought on by frustrated ambition (Carlisle, 1991, pp. 59–86). Mill longed to enter parliament, perhaps to play the part of a 'Girondin' leader in a moderate British revolution; his activities in debating societies and legal studies under Austin were all a preparation for this. His job as a civil servant at India House, which he began in 1823, precluded it. In the 1830s he frequently longed to be in parliament and he compensated by joining the game from the sidelines, attempting to influence events by his political journalism. His article of 1837 on the French republican journalist Armand Carrel is revealing. Carrel was performing the same role as Mill himself: Mill depicts him as 'the greatest political leader of his time', 'a man of action using the press as his instrument', the modern equivalent of the political orators of Athens and Rome and 'a hero

of Plutarch' (*CW*, vol. XX, pp. 170–2, 215). (Plutarch, c.46–c.120 wrote
a series of biographies of classical heroes: they were standard reading
for educated persons from the Renaissance to the end of the nineteenth
century.)

The *Autobiography* projects a self-image of a candid man, always open
to new ideas, never dogmatic about 'philosophic radicalism', nor about
anything else. This image is not entirely true. At the deepest level, Mill
preserved the convictions of his youth, as subsequent chapters will
show. His receptivity to new ideas became highly selective as he grew
older. Some of the best informed commentators have insisted that his
thought was fixed by the time of the *Logic* of 1843 (Robson, 1968,
p. 117). In his later years, he knew about but declined to incorporate
new developments in logic, psychology and political economy which
would render whole swathes of his thought out of date within a few
years of his death (*CW*, vol. XI, pp. lxv, lxxiv–v).

Serious doubts hang over what he writes about Harriet Taylor Mill.
She must have been a remarkable woman, intelligent, committed and
inspirational. But it is difficult to believe that she was as brilliant as Mill
said. Perhaps a man with an over-active moral conscience who alienates
the affections of another man's wife needs to find justifications for what
he has done. The *Autobiography* asserts that his intellectual and moral
development owed more to her than to any other person, and its
rhetoric continually reinforces that message; but the detail contradicts
it. The crucial turning-point of his mental crisis, and the beginnings of
his recovery from that crisis through poetic self-cultivation, occurred
before he met her and apparently owed most to Wordsworth. His critique of the 'abstract' approach of his father, and adoption of a more
'historical' mode of understanding, happened under the impact of
Macaulay, Coleridge, de Tocqueville, Comte, Guizot and others. He
learnt the importance of poetic vision in politics from Carlyle. Packe
and Himmelfarb have said that Harriet was the source of his passion
for liberty; but Rees (1985) has shown that the bones of the essay
On Liberty are to be found in the thought of Bentham and James Mill,
and that many of its arguments are foreshadowed in Mill's writings of
the decade before he met her. He insisted himself that he was already
committed to sexual equality. There is really very little left of the main
lines of his thought that he *could* have derived from her. Maybe, as he
claimed, she pushed him towards socialism: he did not, however, *learn*
about socialism from her, but from the Owenites, Saint-Simonians,
Fourier, Louis Blanc and others. His claims about her influence on him

remain puzzling and unconvincing. He is quite clear that she pushed his *Political Economy* towards socialism in 1848, and his correspondence gives some support to this; but it also demonstrates that events in France at that time had that effect (*CW*, vol. XIII, p. 741; vol. XIV, p. 24). One of his most significant claims was that he owed to her the organizing principle of the book which drew a distinction between the ineluctable laws of production and the changeable laws of distribution. It was this aspect of his reworking of classical political economy which opened the way to a favourable consideration of socialist ideas. But he was already making this distinction in so many words in 1834 (*CW*, vol. V, pp. 225–6). Had she already deeply affected his economic thought, or is this another instance of him exaggerating her influence?

The *Autobiography* is an example of her impact on his published legacy. Without doubt she gave advice at the planning stage – their correspondence proves, for example, that they were obsessed with the need to set the record straight about their premarital relationship. The manuscript of the early draft is covered with her pencil corrections. But the bulk of these are copy-editing, polishing the style. Her substantial changes – which the modern reader is likely to regret – largely take the form of prudent censorship. For example, she paid close attention to remarks about Bentham, removing or toning down passages which referred to his influence on and quarrels with the Mills. She toned down her husband's harsh remarks about his father. She censored several passages where Mill engaged in self-deprecation, thereby reducing the 'confessional' tone and making the final version more detached. None of this alters the overall shape and meaning of the narrative.

If there are questions about the extent of her influence, there are more, raised for example by Packe and Himmelfarb, about whether she was as good for him as he claimed. The period of Mill's marriage was not only the part of his adult life when he published least (though *On Liberty*, *The Subjection of Women*, *Representative Government*, the *Autobiography* and *Utilitarianism* were all drafted then) but also a time of comparative isolation and withdrawal from social and political life. But the low published productivity can perfectly well be explained by illness and exceptional pressure of work at India House. Nor was Mill's isolation entirely Harriet's fault; for example, close friends such as the Flower sisters and John Sterling had died, Mill's enthusiasm for the 1848 revolution in France had upset the Austins, he can hardly be blamed for falling out with Carlyle who took favours and then gossiped spitefully behind his back. Even after Harriet's death Mill was no partygoer. When in parliament he refused Gladstone's dinner invitations on more than one occasion, and expressed his preference for the quiet comforts of home with his stepdaughter to the noisy eulogiums of the world (*CW*, vol. XVI, p. 1048). He wrote to Grote in 1865, 'As for the social influences which so often corrupt or tame men when they go into Parliament, I shall protect myself against those by keeping out of their way' (*CW*, vol. XVI, p. 1096). Mill's occasional avoidance of society was part of his self-image as a critic, outsider and dissident intellectual.

But in spite of this defence it must be admitted that Mill and his wife showed signs of a bunker mentality in the 1850s, coupled with an unpleasing lack of humility. In his New Year's greeting to his wife in 1855, he referred to her as 'the only person living who is worthy to live' (*CW*, vol. XIV, p. 273). Other letters contain what must rank as classics of intellectual arrogance: he referred to their projected writings as 'concentrated thought – a sort of mental pemican, which thinkers, when there are any after us, may nourish themselves with & then dilute for other people' (*CW*, vol. XIV, pp. 112, 141–2).

His letters to Harriet in the 1850s when he was travelling for his health do not always make pleasant reading. Often there is a streak of élitism and even snobbery. Mill persistently grades the people he encounters, for intelligence, cultivation, radicalism and gentility – he even on one occasion remarks on a man who drops his h's, and makes disparaging remarks about northerners. At this time Mill does not appear to be curious about the people he meets, or sympathetic towards them or respectful of them as individuals.

But the bitterness of the correspondence may to some extent be excused by the fact that the couple were seriously ill with TB at this time and convinced that they would soon be dead. 'I look upon it as a piece of excellent good fortune to have the whole summer before one to die in', he wrote in his diary (*CW*, vol. XXVI, p. 665). Perhaps it is unfair to blame Harriet. Perhaps she did not make him like this: perhaps she was the only person to whom he revealed his true self. Still, it is troubling, because otherwise Mill has claims for consideration as a secular saint, a man of generosity and integrity, a hero of European intellectual history, outstanding for the range and nobility of his thought. The sole documented instance of real inhumanity on his part relates to Harriet. His mother and siblings were tardy in paying their respects to her when he announced his engagement in 1851. He thereupon broke off all relations with them. When his mother was dying of cancer of the liver in 1854, he refused in a cruel letter to forgive his sister Mary (who he thought had been especially uncivil to his wife), and visited his mother only once before going abroad.

There is a palpable change in the correspondence after Harriet's death. His letters to his stepdaughter are more agreeable, lightened by whimsy and pleasantry; the affection they express seems healthier. There is less snobbish criticism of others and more generous praise. His pessimism of the 1850s evaporated; 'I do not, as you seem to think, take a gloomy view of human prospects. Few persons look forward to the future career of humanity with more brilliant hopes than I do' (*CW*, vol. XV, p. 843). Eventually he was reconciled with Mary, saving her son when he was in danger of prosecution for fraud. Altogether, we must doubt the *Autobiography*'s account both of the extent and the quality of Harriet's influence.

It is time to return to the question raised in the Introduction of the discursive contexts within which Mill thought. As we have seen, the *Autobiography* places its author centre stage in the evolution of European thought, invoking it to correct alleged deficiencies in English philosophy. Was Mill wrong to attribute so much to German and French historical thinking? Was he more influenced by the philosophical history of the Scottish Enlightenment and of English Whiggism than he cared to admit? After all, the essential idea of his 'Germano-Coleridgeans', namely that any society is a complex entity, bound together by its culture as much as or more than by its formal constitution, is to be found in the thought of that 'Old Whig', Edmund Burke (1729–97). The doctrine that societies move through a succession of stages, and that different institutions are appropriate to each, is found in the writings of eighteenth-century Scots such as Adam Smith, John Millar and Dugald Stewart. Macaulay's celebrated attack on James Mill's *Essay on Government* demands a flexible historical understanding of politics rather than an abstract one. Yet Mill in his *Autobiography* chooses to ignore this; it is the modern French, he insists, who have a philosophy of history, and the modern Germans who have a philosophy of culture.

It is reasonable to assume that Mill had emotional reasons for downplaying British sources. His year in France when he was fourteen was an epoch in his life, a happy emancipation from the discipline of his father. Undoubtedly his love affair with a married woman, and the constant suspicion that 'society' was gossiping about them, helped to alienate him from England. He complained about 'the ponderous dull atmosphere of custom & *respectability*' which weighed upon the English but not upon the French (*CW*, vol. XII p. 192). It was possible to say anything in France, even to attack religion; but the speculations (including free love) of the socialist Fourier (1772–1837) were impossible in 'pinched & methodistical England' (*CW*, vol. XIV, p. 22). An important factor is Mill's radicalism; if that is taken fully into account, it becomes obvious that he would be reluctant to lend any credibility to Whig thought. We must not overlook the disenchantment with his own country which a political animal like Mill feels when, decade after decade, power remains with those he detests.

He disliked the Scottish Enlightenment historian and philosopher Hume for his Tory history and defence of Charles I; Hume was a dishonest man who sold his conscience when he defended the established church (*CW*, vol. XXVI, p. 423). Mill felt no more identity with Whigs; like Bentham, he thought they were just as bad as Tories, and the task of the radicals was to combat 'both the Aristocratic factions' (*CW*, vol. XXIV, p. 799). He was well to the left of the Whig prime ministers of the 1830s, Grey and Melbourne, and even of Brougham and Macaulay, whom he dismissed in a letter to Harriet as 'what all cockneys are, an intellectual dwarf, rounded off and stunted, full grown broad & short, without a germ or principle of further growth in his whole being' (*CW*, vol. XIV, p. 332). He always detested Palmerston (Whig/Liberal prime minister between 1855 and 1865) and to a lesser extent Russell. In spite of all his jeremiads about democracy, he always stood for a considerable extension of the franchise in Britain. As for eighteenth-century philosophy, like his father he found it lacking in seriousness and commitment. The cool, detached stance of Hume or Adam Smith was not for the Mills: 'Is it an evil to have strong convictions, and steady unfluctuating feelings? It is on the contrary, essential to all dignity or solidity of character, and to all fitness for guiding or governing mankind' (*CW*, vol. XXII, p. 294). He thought that the great Whig quarterly, the *Edinburgh Review*, lacked earnestness (*CW*, vol. XII, p. 312). There are clear ideological differences, then, setting Mill apart from English Whiggism.

The shifting location of his allegiance and identity is similarly to be explained in terms of political ideology, for Mill was political to the core of his being. As a young man he thought that France, thanks to her Revolution, and democratic America were the happiest and most virtuous nations on earth (*CW*, vol. XXVI, p. 453). France was the laboratory of modern society, therefore French history was the most interesting, English one of the least (*CW*, vol. XIV, pp. 6, 32). Tocqueville's work diminished his enthusiasm for America, but the Civil War, which for Mill was a crusade against slavery, and the triumph of the North in that conflict, completely restored it. He continued to think that the French peasantry who had gained the land in the Revolution were the happiest people in Europe (*CW*, vol. XXIV, p. 1004). Through his reading he lived in the classical past as well as in the nineteenth century, and he identified strongly with democratic Athens. Athens stood for civilization; the Spartans, 'those hereditary Tories and Conservatives of Greece' (*CW*, vol. XI, p. 303) and the aristocratic Romans stood for barbarism (*CW*, vol. XXV, p. 1097; vol. XI, pp. 313, 321–5).

But why did he think that he could only get a philosophy of history from continental sources? It is well known that Adam Smith and others had developed the theory of four great stages in historical evolution: the hunter-gathering, pastoral, agricultural and commercial, each stage having a corresponding set of social and political institutions, of manners and ideas. Why does Mill ignore this in the *Autobiography*, and lavish praise on the Saint-Simonians, for the 'connected view which they for the first time presented to me, of the natural order of human progress' (CW, vol. I, p. 171)? One answer is that the philosophy of history Mill was looking for was an *idealist* one, and that was exactly what the Saint-Simonians, and Comte, and indeed the 'Germano-Coleridgeans' provided. That of the Scottish historical school, with its emphasis upon great economic stages, was much more materialist. For Mill, progress is not driven on by sex or money (by population pressures and economic developments, as Smith, Malthus and Marx thought) nor yet by the lust for power: lusts of various kinds hold progress back. The advance of humanity is a consequence of the advance of knowledge in which the rational element triumphs over the animal.

Mill provides another answer himself. He identifies three stages in the evolution of historical thought: in the first, the historian transports present feelings and notions back into the past; in the second, the historian attempts to look at the past with its own eyes; in the third, the historian constructs a science of history (*CW*, vol. XX, pp. 222–3). The failing of eighteenth-century, therefore of most Whig, historical and social thinking in Mill's view is that it is still in the first stage; and the third stage, scientific history, is impossible before the second has been attained. Imprisoned in the perspectives of its own age, the attitude of British historical writing to the past was too negative and critical; it failed to achieve sympathetic understanding – for example, it failed to do justice to the civilizing achievements of the Catholic church in the Middle Ages. The second stage is anticipated in the historical novels of Scott, and achieved in the histories of Niebuhr, Carlyle, Michelet, and later Grote, who enables the reader to understand what it was like to be a classical Greek. The beginnings of the third stage can be found in the writings of Guizot.

To an extent then Mill is right to stress continental thought, and up to a point his *Autobiography* is a sound history of his own ideas. But the essential philosophical idea, with crucial implications for social and political thought, is that societies are organic wholes which evolve through stages and that different institutions are appropriate to different periods; and Scottish historical thinking of the eighteenth century had already proposed this theory. In other writings Mill admits this, praising Kames and Ferguson, Brown and Reid, Smith and even Hume, and especially Millar, whose historical speculations were similar to Guizot's (*CW*, vol. XIII, p. 683). And if one turns from Mill's historical and social philosophy to his philosophy in general, it is perfectly clear that the essential core, indeed the great bulk of the theory in the *Logic* and the *Political Economy*, is British in inspiration.

If the *Autobiography* distorts Mill's mental evolution, it is more seriously at fault as a history of European ideas. To be sure, Mill's mistake has been widely shared; the idea that the eighteenth-century Enlightenment was unhistorical has enjoyed a wide and lengthy currency, and no doubt Mill's writings played some part in disseminating it. The charge would undoubtedly be true if Mill had directed it mainly at his father and Bentham, whose thought is lamentably unhistorical (Robson, 1968, p. 46). But a widespread error is none the less an error, and it is utterly false to claim, as Mill does in his essay on Coleridge, that the *philosophes* held history in disrespect, that before Herder and Michelet there was no attempt to write a history which was 'a science of causes and effects' in which 'the facts and events of the past have a meaning and an intelligible place in the gradual evolution of humanity', and that the 'Germano-Coleridgeans' were the first to produce 'a philosophy of society ... a contribution, the largest made by any class of thinkers, towards the philosophy of human culture' (*CW*, vol. X, p. 139). In these sentences the eighteenth-century achievements of Montesquieu, Rousseau, Ferguson, Hume, Smith, Millar and Gibbon are ignored. This distortion is required by the dramatic structure of his narrative of his own life, which stages the eighteenth century and the modern age as central players, antagonists whose conflict and reconciliation give the plot its meaning. When considering Mill's claims for the influence of continental thought upon him, we must be clear that 'continental' largely means 'French'. In spite of his obeisances to Germany, his knowledge of German thought was limited and mostly indirect or in translation. He was never as much of a Germanist as his British contemporaries Coleridge, Carlyle, G.H. Lewes or George Eliot, and some of the profounder ideas of German social and historical thinking passed him by.

Mill's narrative, then, has subtle distortions at the core of its structure. It also leaves a great deal out. Notoriously it never mentions his mother, acknowledging his father alone: 'I was born ... the eldest son of James Mill'. His mother *did* figure in the early draft, where he criticized her inappropriately and unjustly: 'That rarity in England, a really warm hearted mother, would in the first place have made my father a totally different being, and in the second would have made the children grow up loving and being loved' (*CW*, vol. I, p. 612). There is independent evidence to confirm that Mrs Mill lacked all distinction: Francis Place commented that she was vain and girlish and had no mind in her body, and Mrs Grote told that '[James Mill] married a stupid woman, a housemaid of a woman, and left off caring for her and treated her as his squah but was always faithful to her' (Packe, 1954, pp. 32–3). But this is no excuse for Mill's uncharacteristic lapse into antifeminism, blaming his mother for his father's coldness and irritability and for the deficiencies of his childhood. The fact that a man who came to dislike and despise his mother wrote a feminist classic gives cause for thought.

It is not at all surprising that an *Autobiography* written in the Victorian age makes no mention of its subject's sexual life. Still, we would like to know about it, for it might help to explain his obsessive Malthusianism, and his relations with his wife and mother. Freud remarked that the *Autobiography* was 'so prudish or so etherial that one could never gather from it that human beings consist of men and women' (Jones, 1953, vol. I, pp. 191–2). He does not tell us about his personal finances, nor about his second nervous breakdown at the time of his father's death, the illness which left him with a permanent facial twitch. His professional life of twenty-five years in the East India Office gets barely a mention, and the book lacks almost all sense of place; of all the houses and neighbourhoods in which Mill lived, only Forde Abbey is described.

For this is a pure intellectual biography, a life of the spirit whose major protagonists are books and ideas. It presents a man as a disembodied mind, whose concrete, animal existence is not worthy of mention. Leslie Stephen remarked that the book contained no affectionate remarks

about anybody but Harriet, and it is true that it makes Mill seem somewhat isolated, giving us little sense of his sociability and social context.
It makes him appear very self-absorbed, inward-turning, and perhaps
this was an aspect of his personality. After a day in 1855 walking in the
volcanic scenery around Naples he wrote to Harriet that he was truly
enjoying the beauty now, in his head, in his bedroom by candlelight
(*CW*, vol. XIV, p. 322). At this period of his life he often addressed
Harriet in his letters in the third person – 'she', 'her' – and Packe cites
this as evidence of his uxorious deference. It may, rather, mean that he
is not in fact addressing his wife at all but instead communing with
himself *about* her.

The reader of the *Autobiography* is left dissatisfied, feeling that only
a part of the man has been revealed. What was the mundane, everyday
John Stuart Mill like? An attempt to complete the portrait would go
behind the ultra-modern image Mill supplied of himself to show the
stoic and classicist, sitting on top of the ruins of the baths of Caligula
with John Sterling, looking in rapture at the ruins of ancient Rome.
It would tell of his country walks, twenty miles or more a day at five
miles an hour, performing mathematical problems and botanizing as
he walked. It would tell of his professional life, arriving in his office to
breakfast on a boiled egg and tea, taking nothing else for the rest of
the working day, composing his despatches and reports as he walked
up and down his large bare office, writing them standing at a tall writing desk. It would not omit the hours he spent at the piano, sometimes
improvising his own compositions. It would show that, apart from the
period of withdrawal in the 1840s and 1850s, he was good company,
loved by his friends, light-hearted and with a sense of humour. Mill
thought of himself as a gentleman, but he supported working men candidates for parliament, advised them on their reading and lent them
books. It would not ignore his gifts to charity – half his estate was left to
the cause of women's education. It would show his kindness, for example to the young German classicist Gomperz who, depressed at having
been rejected by Mill's stepdaughter, persistently failed to produce
promised translations of Mill's writings; or to his colleague Thornton,
whom he saved from the sack by doing his work for a whole year when
Thornton was suffering from depression. It would reveal his passion for
foreign travel, going with his stepdaughter around Greece and Turkey
in 1862, living in the tents they carried with them. The *Autobiography*,
then, leaves much out and subtly distorts what it includes so as to
enhance the meaning of what was already a meaningful life.

3

LOGIC AND POLITICAL ECONOMY

Mill's fundamental philosophical ideas are contained in *A System of Logic*, which came out in 1843, and in two works published in 1865: *Auguste Comte and Positivism* and *An Examination of Sir William Hamilton's Philosophy*, where at great length Mill annihilates a philosopher who would otherwise be forgotten. The *Principles of Political Economy*, published in 1848, was begun in late 1845 and finished in early 1847. That a closely reasoned and information-packed book of 450,000 words should be written in so short a time is astonishing, the more so in view of the fact that Mill spent six of those months writing forty-three leaders for the *Morning Chronicle* on the Irish potato famine, and continued to fulfil his duties at India House. Mill revised the book for the second and third editions of 1849 and 1852 so as to give a more sympathetic discussion of socialism. There were five further editions in Britain in Mill's lifetime, plus a cheap People's edition. It was the standard textbook in economics for half a century, attracted a wide general readership and influenced British politics: together with the *Logic* it laid the foundations of Mill's reputation as a serious thinker. In fact, Mill's most creative and original work as an economist is in his four *Essays on Some Unsettled Questions of Political Economy*, written by 1830 but not published until 1844.

The *Logic*

Mill's aims as a philosopher are standard Enlightenment ones, conceived under the aegis of the idea and ideal of science. For this reason he thought of himself as a *positivist*, sharing many doctrines with his friend Auguste Comte. Mill intends, first of all, to explain and justify the methods of science. Then he wishes to furnish a scientific account of the mind and its workings. He is a 'thoroughgoing naturalist' (Skorupski, 1989, p. 5) – he believes that human beings and their minds are natural phenomena, to be explained in substantially the same way that scientists explain the natural world – that is to say in terms of cause and effect, just as we explain planetary motions and chemical reactions. Mill, together with his father and Bentham, believed that a perfected human science would clear up political disputes and support the aims of 'philosophic radicalism'. Today, his faith in the power of science to resolve ideological disputes at all, let alone to resolve them in the direction he desired, looks distinctly implausible and did so by the latter part of the nineteenth century. By then his economic science was challenged by Marx's, and his environmentalism, which defended racial and sexual equality, seemed outmoded by the side of a Social Darwinism which insisted that the races and the sexes were not equal.

The foundation stone of his thought is the associationist psychology which he inherited from John Locke (1632–1704), David Hume (1711–76) and Hartley, and most immediately from his father's *Analysis of the Phenomena of the Human Mind* of 1829. Mill thought that psychology, the science of mind, had essentially been perfected in that book (James Mill had written, 'If I had time to write a book I would make the human mind as plain as the road from Charing Cross to St. Paul's') (Thomas, 1979, p. 121). The Mills thought that the mind could be explained in terms of a few simple laws. All the contents of the mind, all knowledge, comes from experience, most of it via the five senses, but some also being experience of our bodily states, such as pleasures and pains. Then there is the law of memory: the mind has the ability to call up an idea of sensations and feelings, or groups of these, which it has experienced in the past. Next come the *laws of association*, in accordance with which the mind associates together its ideas, whether they be present experiences or memories. First, an idea tends to be associated with and to call up in memory ideas which it resembles (for example, the sight of a swan's neck calls up the idea of a snake). Second, when a number of ideas have often been experienced or thought of simultaneously or in quick succession (for example, thunder and lightning, or the ideas of colour, shape, smell, etc. which go to make up the complex idea of an orange) the experience of one of the component ideas is associated with and may call up the others. Third, associations will be stronger if one of the ideas is particularly intense; for example, the sight of a candle will vividly recall the memory of the pain of touching the flame (*CW*, vol. VIII, p. 852). Fourth, certain ideas may be associated together so pervasively and strongly that the mind becomes incapable of separating them. For example, we cannot think of things without relating them spatially in a certain way, simply because we have always experienced them in a particular spatial framework. Mill calls this 'chemical association'; the component ideas become so fused as to lose their separate identities, rather as sodium and chlorine, which are poisonous, become nutritious when chemically compounded into salt. But our inseparable associations are not necessarily true or universal; we cannot conceive of two straight lines enclosing a space, but they might do so on another planet (*CW*, vol. XIV, p. 29). It should be mentioned in passing that by the end of his life Mill's associationism was becoming out of date; psychologists were increasingly interested in the physiological basis of mind which Mill's theory, in spite of his enthusiasm for the work of his younger colleague Alexander Bain, largely ignores.

Mill's *a posteriori* philosophy, in accordance with which all knowledge is *posterior* to, derived from experience, is not 'pure'; it has a political purpose. He criticizes his philosophical contemporaries, Sir William Hamilton in *An Examination of Sir William Hamilton's Philosophy*, and William Whewell in the *Logic* as representatives of what he calls the intuitive or 'a priori' school in philosophy. Intuitivists argue that certain truths, truths of the utmost importance, are known directly and immediately, *prior* to or in addition to particular experiences. An intuitivist might say for example that whereas a series of experiences enables me to conclude that swans are white and that iron rusts when wet, I do not need any evidence to know that I am a coherent self, having a mind which knows an external, material world, that I am free to choose between good and evil and that it is my duty to tell the truth and to love and serve God. These truths are as it were inbuilt, or known by a kind of sixth sense, or are self-evident in the sense that their opposites are inconceivable or utterly unbelievable. So my conviction that swans are white can be controverted if someone shows me a black swan: but no evidence can be brought against my knowledge of God and of my fundamental duties. We just *know* these things, directly and intuitively.

Mill believes that intuitivism is at once irrational, and a bastion of conservatism in morals and politics. It makes opinions their own proof, and feelings their own justification.

By the aid of this theory, every inveterate belief and every intense feeling, of which the origin is not remembered, is enabled to

dispense with the obligation of justifying itself by reason. ...There
never was such an instrument devised for consecrating all deep
seated prejudices (*CW*, vol. I, p. 233).

Associationism shows how beliefs can appear intuitively certain even
if they are not true; if women have always been seen in subjection to
men, then that experience will be stamped upon the mind and wifely
subjection will seem inevitable and natural. Mill thinks that if any
appeal to intuitive knowledge is ruled out, and if all are compelled to
justify their beliefs scientifically and back them up with properly
analysed evidence, then conservatism will be undermined and moral
and political progress promoted.

Mill's *Logic* has a second political target, for he felt the need of a
decisive reply to Macaulay's attack on his father. To Mill, Macaulay was
a conservative, and his conservatism was not unlike that of the old
Whig Edmund Burke. Like Burke, Macaulay argued against radicals
and revolutionaries by appealing to *experience*. Mill appeals to experience as well, so how does he differ? Macaulay and Burke championed
experience as opposed to *abstract theory*; and, to Macaulay, James Mill
and Bentham were perfect examples of abstract theorists. They used
the principle of utility to condemn the existing order and propose
sweeping changes. Far better, Macaulay thought, to proceed with caution, relying on concrete historical knowledge; the statesman should
always keep in touch with the known facts. Mill's reply is that experience and theory must go hand-in-hand. He calls Macaulay's approach
'the Experimental, or Chemical, mode of investigation' (*CW*, vol. XVIII,
p. 878) and argues that it is incapable of providing scientific explanations of politics and society, as we shall see.

At the heart of Mill's logic is a theory of the method of science; and
this is framed as a discussion of inductive and deductive reasoning.
To Mill, deductive reasoning meant *syllogistic* reasoning, as it had to
logicians since Aristotle created their discipline in the fourth century BC.
After Mill's death, his godson Bertrand Russell and Frege carried the
subject forward so dramatically as to expel the syllogistic logic of
Aristotle and Mill from the textbooks and consign it to history – but
that need not concern us. A syllogism has a major premise and a minor
premise, and from these the conclusion is deduced. The major premise
takes the form of a general or universal statement, as in the textbook
example, 'All men are mortal'. The minor premise will be a less general
or a specific statement, such as 'Socrates is a man'. From these the valid

conclusion follows, 'Therefore Socrates is mortal.' Deductive reasoning, then, begins with a *general* statement, and infers a *particular* conclusion. Induction by contrast begins with *particular* statements and infers a *general* conclusion. I collect a series of particular observation statements, let us say about kettles of water coming to the boil when heated to 100°C. From these I infer the general statement that 'water boils at 100°C'. So it appears that there are two kinds of inference, deductive (from generals to particulars) and inductive (from particulars to generals). Mill maintains however that there is a third species of reasoning which is the foundation of the other two (*CW*, vol. VII, p. 162).

He argues that all inference is from particulars to particulars. I put my finger in the fire and experience intense pain; from this I infer that if I put my finger into the candle flame I shall again be hurt. This in essence is what reasoning is all about, and in this sense babies and dogs reason, as well as philosophers. Reasoning is from case to like case (*CW*, vol. VII, pp. 186–92). I witness the death of Socrates, and then of Plato; from these experiences I infer that Aristotle will die. Furthermore I can infer that Tom will die, Dick will die, Harry will die and so on. I can sum up all of these inferences in the general proposition, 'all men are mortal'. I can then use this general proposition to abbreviate and simplify the process of reasoning in the future, casting my argument in deductive form, 'All men are mortal, the Duke of Wellington is a man, therefore the Duke of Wellington is mortal'. It now looks as if I have deduced my conclusion from a general statement, but, Mill insists, this simply masks the real process of inference which is going on. The syllogism about the Duke of Wellington is really a shorthand form for 'Tom was a man and he died, Dick was a man and he died, Harry was a man and he died...therefore the Duke of Wellington, who is a man, will die.' In effect, Mill has undermined the distinction between induction and deduction; but his theory is closer to the received view of induction and so it comes as no surprise that Mill claims that 'Deductive or Demonstrative Sciences are all, without exception, Inductive Sciences' (*CW*, vol. VII, p. 253).

Most subsequent philosophy has not accepted Mill's theory. Few would accept that 'All inference is from particulars to particulars' (*CW*, vol. VII, p. 193); most would insist that deductive inference *can* simply be from generals to particulars. So why does Mill want to rule this out? What worries him is the notion that a piece of deductive reasoning might be valid, might yield true knowledge, even if it began from a general assertion which could not be proved by reference to experience.

So, for example, the assertion 'all men are mortal' cannot be proved experientially because we cannot have experience of all men, past, present and to come. Likewise 'parallel lines, if extended to infinity, will never meet'; we cannot experience infinity, nor all possible pairs of parallel lines. Such assertions, when used as first premises in deductive inference, are postulated, taken for granted without evidence. And this of course is *a priori* reasoning, exactly the path to 'truth' which Mill wishes to banish.

This helps explain why Mill adopts an attitude towards the use of hypotheses in scientific reasoning which few if any present-day scientists and philosophers of science would accept. Science advances by proposing hypotheses which fit the observed facts. If a hypothesis fits well and explains a great deal, it is accepted as true – until new facts turn up which will not fit, or a new hypothesis is proposed which is even more successful and all-embracing. Success and good coverage count as proof, and indeed are often the only possible proof, as when physicists theorize about entities – quarks, black holes – which can never be observed. Mill does not accept this. He thinks that hypotheses are useful in the process of scientific discovery, but that they remain mere conjectures until they have been validated inductively, proved conclusively by reference to observed facts (*CW*, vol. VII, p. 483; vol. XXI, p. 236; vol. XI, p. 350). One reason for this exacting standard, which if accepted would fatally handicap scientific inquiry, is that a scientific edifice which consisted mainly of good hypotheses could not have the certainty and finality which Mill wanted. Another reason is once again his determination to exclude *a priori* reasoning. A hypothesis looks to him too much like something accepted prior to and independently of observation. A lax attitude towards hypotheses might open the way to the intuitive claims he wishes to undermine. Mill's insistence on conclusive evidence is one of the most fundamental characteristics of his mind, hence he praises the eighteenth-century idealist philosopher Bishop Berkeley (1685–1753) for 'the most memorable lesson ever given to mankind ... of not believing without evidence' (*CW*, vol. XI, p. 452). His stance on this issue has far-reaching consequences for his thought, as we shall see.

The main business of science, according to Mill, is to discover, by induction, causal laws. Eventually, the system of scientific knowledge will be complete, taking the form of causal laws at different levels of generality. These laws, though all discovered by induction, will be connected together in a system having a deductive form which, as explained above, abbreviates and summarizes the process of inductive reasoning. Mill has a conception of what a perfected science would look like, derived from the model of Sir Isaac Newton's physics. Simplicity and generality are the keywords: science seeks to explain the observed complexity of the world in terms of a small number of ultimate laws, just as Newton explained the heavens, the tides and motion by his laws of gravity. As Mill puts it, 'What are the fewest and simplest assumptions, which being granted, the whole existing order of nature would result?' (*CW*, vol. VII, p. 317; vol. XXXI, p. 95). Moreover, the greater our success in connecting our scientific knowledge into a coherent deductive system, the greater our assurance that the individual components of that knowledge are correct.

Over half of Book 6 of the *Logic* is devoted to social science, or sociology; and a principal purpose of this discussion is to resolve the controversy between James Mill and Macaulay about method. Mill terms his father's method the 'geometrical, or abstract method'; he calls Macaulay's the 'chemical, or experimental method'. He rejects both, proposing instead the 'physical, or concrete deductive method', and the 'inverse deductive, or historical method'. The essential fact about societies is their complexity and diversity. For this reason it might seem that Macaulay's empirical method is appropriate. For Macaulay starts from the postulate that human affairs are complex, therefore the abstract deductive method of the utilitarians which assumes that men are always and everywhere the same, will not do. Experience for Macaulay is the key; we must know societies in their rich specificity and refuse to cram them into some over-simple theoretical straightjacket. Humans become transformed in the ever-varying circumstances of social life. This is like Mill's account of the chemical method. The behaviour of chemical compounds, Mill thinks, cannot be explained in terms of a few simple laws, because compounds are in a sense new and unlike their constituent parts. For example, water, which puts out fire, is quite unlike its constituent parts hydrogen and oxygen, which when mixed burn with great ferocity. From a knowledge of the elements it would be impossible to deduce the behaviour of the compounds, and so the chemist relies upon observation and experiment.

Mill denies that this method is appropriate in sociology. In the first place the social scientist cannot, unlike the chemist, conduct experiments. Second, human affairs are much more complex than chemicals. In chemical investigations it is possible to isolate factors and correlate them and in this way to discover empirical laws of cause and effect; this cannot be done in social inquiries. For example, if we identify a number of prosperous nations, all of which have a policy of protective tariffs, we cannot conclude that the protective tariffs cause the prosperity. Prosperity might result from a complex intermixture of causes, and the mixture might be different in every case.

On the other hand, the geometrical or abstract method will not do. Mill's examples of attempts to apply this to society are Hobbes and the Benthamites. Hobbes supposed that political behaviour could be deduced from fear, the Benthamites from the maxim that humans act in accordance with their interests. Mill rightly insists that human behaviour is not all caused by a single motive. He goes along with Macaulay to the extent of admitting that James Mill attempted to explain the human mind in terms of too few causes (*CW*, vol. XXXI, p. 103).

For this reason, the physical, or concrete deductive method comes nearer the mark. Mill's conception of this method is patterned upon Newtonian mechanics. We do not explain the orbit of a planet in terms of one cause or force, but by the *composition of forces*; we deduce the effect of the force of gravity, then of the centrifugal force, combine them and this yields the orbit. This method is better adapted to the complexity of social affairs. Nevertheless, in most departments of sociology it cannot be applied. For in social science we are concerned, not with the operation of one or two causes, but with the interaction of many; and the combined operation of several causes cannot be predicted with any hope of certainty. Mill knows of only one department of social science where the physical method is appropriate (though he leaves open the possibility that more may be discovered) and that is political economy. Economic behaviour is peculiar in that it can largely be explained in terms of a very small number of causes or laws.

For other areas, the right method in Mill's view (he attributes this insight to Comte) is the inverse deductive or historical method. This is a kind of half-way house between deductive explanation and the inductive discovery of empirical laws. The observation of society, both by the ordinary practical person and by the more systematic social inquirer, yields a stock of unproven generalizations – such as that representative institutions, in an advanced commercial society, produce good government. As already remarked, these generalizations cannot be validated by induction alone, for the contributing factors are too numerous to isolate. The way forward therefore is to validate them by attempting to deduce them from already known general laws of human nature – for example, from the principles of psychology. This then is a deductive method, but it is inverse because it commences from observation and low-level empirical generalizations instead of from higher-level laws; and it proves the empirical generalizations by finding their laws, instead of proving the laws by showing that the generalizations deduced from them fit the facts.

Mill thought this was the appropriate method for the science of *ethology*. The most fundamental of the human sciences, in his view, was psychology, which explained the unvarying laws of the individual mind. Next in order would come ethology. Ethology would discover the laws of the formation of character. They would explain how the laws of psychology, working in conjunction with different combinations of circumstances, produced individual and national characters of different types. Ethology, then, is the science of human nature, explaining how it comes to be and how it varies from time to time and from place to place. It would form the basis of sociology in all its branches – the sciences of the laws of social interaction, of politics and of history. The science of ethology is necessary for Mill because, like other Associationists, he believes that humans are malleable. Just as knowledge comes from experience, so experience forms character. Again, like many other Associationists (especially the eighteenth-century French *philosophe* Helvétius), Mill presents the malleability doctrine in egalitarian form. Men and women are not born unequal in abilities and character; inequalities are environmentally produced. Not even genius needs to be 'a rare gift bestowed on few. By the aid of suitable culture all might possess it, though in unequal degrees' (*CW*, vol. I, p. 334). Accordingly, Mill will not believe claims that there are genetic racial differences. Racial differences could all be explained by social conditioning (*CW*, vol. XXIV, p. 891). This is not to say that Mill thinks there is no given, unchanging human nature. Not everything is subject to environmental determination: 'Men, however, in a state of society, are still men; their actions and passions are obedient to the laws of individual human nature' (*CW*, vol. VIII, p. 879). The laws of association are universal, and so are the capacities to feel pleasure and pain.

I have now explained the central core of Mill's philosophy, and it is time to look at some of the beliefs and theories that flow from it. This will help us understand it better: it will also bring out a number of problems and difficulties. First we might mention his theory of the nature of mathematical knowledge. It would have been possible for him to agree with the Scottish philosopher Dugald Stewart (1753–1828), and with many later philosophers and mathematicians, in thinking that mathematical sciences are formal sciences evolved by the mind out of its own abstract conceptions, and that they are not about the real world of experience at all: but he does not. Stewart's theory raises a problem: if maths is a creation of the mind, then why is it so powerful in scientific explanations of the world? But above all, of course, the conception of mathematics as a purely formal science is unacceptable to Mill because it would mean that mathematics is *a priori*, independent of experience. This would be the thin end of the wedge, opening the way for *a priori* knowledge in other areas – of our duty to obey our social superiors, of women to obey men and so on. Mill therefore insists that mathematics, like physics or chemistry, is an inductive science; we discover its truths by observation. But if the formal account of mathematics creates difficulties, so does Mill's inductive one. For example, if mathematical axioms are derived from experience, then why is it ridiculous to check whether there are any bent straight lines? And if we derive our knowledge of the truth that $2+3=5$ from experience, then why is it so difficult to imagine any experience which could prove it wrong? It appears to be the type of an intuitive truth; self-evident, a proposition whose contrary is absurd. Mill's reply would be that it is a case of inseparable or chemical association; we have so persistently experienced $2+3$ equalling 5 that the association has become unbreakable.

Mill's determination to believe nothing unless proved by observation, and the very limited role he accords to hypotheses, explains something which has puzzled many commentators – his less than complete endorsement of Darwin's theory of evolution by natural selection. Mill is simply being consistent with his methodological protocols: 'In regard to the Darwinian hypothesis ... Darwin ... has shown that it is capable of accounting for vastly more than had been supposed ... though it is not proved to be the origin of the organic world we now see' (*CW*, vol. XVII, pp. 1553–4). Strictly speaking, Mill is correct: but twentieth-century scientists would count the power of Darwin's hypothesis to account for so much as sufficient proof.

Mill's thoughts on religion partly follow from this also. Given the deficit of proof suffered by all religions, Mill had to be an agnostic. Actually, his stance was less cool than that word suggests; though he admired Christ as depicted in the New Testament, and the mid-century Oxford Movement for its attempt to bring Christianity back to its original ideals (*CW*, vol. XXIV, p. 814), he detested established Christianity, going so far as to call it 'a child of the devil' (*CW*, vol. XIV, p. 92). This was partly because the established church upheld the established order, with all its injustices; partly because Mill thought that the 'morality' taught in the Old Testament was barbaric and *im*moral (for example, the idea of God visiting the sins of the fathers upon innocent children) (*CW*, vol. XIV, p. 53). Mill thought that the time was not ripe for publishing his hostility to religion; if he did, few would listen to him on any other subject. But his warmth on this issue is apparent in his private correspondence, for example with Comte. Some of his friends were therefore surprised and disappointed when his essay on 'Theism' was published posthumously in 1874, for he there left open the possibility, not only of the existence of God but also of Christ's special mission from God and of life after death. But once again, *we* should not be surprised, given Mill's doctrines on belief and proof. If the existence of God, Christ's mission, and immortality cannot be proved, neither can they be disproved; and therefore it is rational to retain an open mind. Given the existence of evil in the world however, and the sufferings of the innocent, Mill never thought it rational to entertain the possibility of a God who is at once completely good and all-powerful. Unless we suppose that God is bad, or indifferent, we must conclude that his power to do good and prevent evil is limited.

Given Mill's enthusiasm for science, his resolve to believe nothing unwarranted by experience leads him to a dissonant conclusion. All my experience is of ideas, originally of *phenomena* as Mill terms them – sensations of redness, hardness, sweetness, roundness, etc. But these phenomena are mental, in my mind. The consequences of thinking this come out in Mill's critique of Hamilton. Hamilton argues that all perception is dual, involving an immediate consciousness of a mind which perceives, and of an external, material world which is perceived. In all perception there is an intuitive knowledge of mind and matter (*CW*, vol. IX, p. 150). Mill, as usual, denies that there is any intuitive knowledge apart from experience; but since all experience is of phenomena internal to the mind, what happens to matter? Mill denies that we have any knowledge of, or warrant for believing in, a material reality external to sensation: 'I do not believe that the real externality to us of anything, except other minds, is capable of proof' (*CW*, vol. IX, p. 187n). He has therefore been labelled a 'phenomenalist'; he refers to himself as a Berkelian idealist, after Berkeley who argued that nothing exists except minds and ideas.

The man on the Clapham omnibus will be astonished that so hard-headed a man as Mill comes to a conclusion so contrary to common sense; but once again it follows from his methodological beliefs.

An escape from this trap would be possible if he accorded an enhanced role to hypothesis in knowledge. If I cannot prove that there is an external, material world, at the very least the existence of such a world is a good hypothesis which explains the facts of experience well, perhaps better than any other hypothesis. For most of us this is enough.

The argument which made Mill think he could not prove the existence of matter also made him think he could not prove the existence of the self. As Hume pointed out a century earlier, if all I experience, all I can be certain of, is a series of sensations, then when I look for myself, all I find is that series. If I cannot know a material world external to sensations, in exactly the same way I cannot know a self enduring through and apart from sensations. Mill's phenomenalism implies this, yet there seems to be something profoundly wrong with it: my awareness is not just of a collection of sensations, but of a collection which is *mine*. Mill feels this profound wrongness, but admits he can find no way out of the *impasse*: 'The truth is, that we are here face to face with that final inexplicability' (*CW*, vol. IX, p. 194). Obviously he will not take an intuitivist's way out, contending that the sense of self is prior to or accompanies experience. His problem with the self is surprising in one who condemned the Benthamite school for ignoring self-culture, and who praised that 'Germano-Coleridgean school' which made the self the first principle of all knowledge. His reaction against Benthamism did not leave as much as a scratch on the deeper levels of his philosophy.

According to Alexander Bain, when Mill had finished his *Logic*, he wished to move on to the science of ethology. This was an obvious thing for him to do. He thought his father had established the fundamentals of psychology; ethology was the next human science in order. Until that task was done, a well-founded social science would be impossible. But, as Bain tells us, Mill made no progress, gave up the attempt, and turned to writing his *Political Economy* instead (Bain, 1882, pp. 78–9). The failure of Mill's projected ethology raises fascinating questions about his conception of the moral sciences and may reveal fundamental problems. Remember, Mill thought that the human sciences, like the natural ones, advanced by the discovery of causal laws. He gives an example of the kind of causal explanation ethology might yield; it can be summed up as 'Experience tends to produce caution' (*CW*, vol. VIII, p. 862). This seems plausible, but as an example of what ethology can do, it is none too impressive; it hardly looks like a discovery. Physics advances by going beyond common sense, showing for example that the earth revolves around the sun. It has yet to be shown that our understanding of human behaviour can be completely transformed in this way.

More profoundly, we might question the initial assumption of positivism and doubt whether the methods and concepts of natural science are appropriate when studying human behaviour. Mill knew that the 'moral sciences' had not got very far, but apparently thought this was because they were 'just very much more complicated' (Winch, 1963, p. 72). Perhaps the difference is not one of degree, but of kind. In this century the most important form of doubt about positivism has been the *hermeneutic* theory, associated for example with the historian and philosopher R.G. Collingwood (1889–1943), that human behaviour must be *understood* in terms of *reasons* rather than *explained* in terms of *causes*. In causal accounts, we explain an action by referring it to the general, causal law which we believe has determined it; hence we group it with other like actions. In hermeneutic accounts, we understand an action by discovering the reasons for it, and this is essentially the same kind of thing as understanding a conversation; moreover, each conversation is different from every other. Hermeneutic accounts are narratives, which tell the story of how the action came about. Narratives are detailed; each one tracks a unique series of happenings and this marks them off from scientific explanations which seek general patterns.

Hermeneutics rests upon a sense of the centrality of *language*. If we take this idea seriously, we might also doubt Mill's belief in universal psychological laws. He thought that psychology came first, before the social sciences; first we explain the individual human mind, then we go on to explain social interaction with the help of psychological laws – for example the laws of association – which we have discovered. But language is a social product and primarily a mode of social interaction so, according to Mill's theory of the order of the sciences, the science of psychology should make no reference to it. Sensation and association would be pre-linguistic (*CW*, vol. VIII, p. 664). But perhaps this is wrong; perhaps language goes all the way down, affecting the way we perceive the world (after all, as any parent knows, a child does not distinguish colours as adults do until it learns to *name* them). If this is so, then since languages vary, perception and association will vary too, and in this sense will be social products.

These may seem abstruse philosophical considerations: but they have practical, political implications. Insofar as they undermine Mill's positivist faith in social science, they also undermine his élitist belief in social scientific experts. If the central activity is understanding language and narratives, then definitive answers will be elusive; new shades of meaning wait to be discovered in the word, the sentence and the story. Therefore the interpretation offered by the man on the Clapham omnibus, though it may not be as good as that of the professor in his study, will at least have some rival validity because it has the advantage of an alternative point of view.

The *Principles of Political Economy*

The reader should not take these criticisms of Mill's positivism as conclusive; philosophers are still debating these issues. And there is at least one area – as Mill himself would have insisted – where the social scientific ambition appears to have been realized, namely the science of economics, or as he calls it 'Political Economy'. This is just a little bit odd, from Mill's point of view; according to his theory of the order of the sciences, it ought to be necessary first to perfect ethology, the science of the formation of individuals, before going on to explain how those individuals interact in economic life. But Mill thought that economics was an exception, in that it was possible to ignore the diversity of human character which ethology would explore. Economic theories can be constructed on the assumption that economic agents are rational calculators of self-interest who wish to maximize their gains with the minimum of effort. Mill recognizes that this is a simplification: many individuals are not, or not entirely, like that. But it is sufficiently close to the truth to yield correct results when our object of study is the mass, the economic system as a whole (*CW*, vol. V, pp. 321, 325–6). Or it provides us with a set of laws which can be combined with varying circumstances in order to explain a diversity of economies.

Before outlining Mill's economics, a structuring assumption must be mentioned. Like other 'Classical Political Economists' – for example, Adam Smith and David Ricardo (and Karl Marx) – Mill organizes his account of the economic system around three factors of production: natural resources (land, minerals etc.), capital, and labour. This yields three different kinds of income – rent, interest and wages – and may or may not yield a three-class model of society, with landlords, capitalists and labourers.

Again, like other classical political economists, Mill has a theory of *value* which determines *price* but is not the same as price. Prices may rise with inflation, as money becomes more available and therefore cheaper, but this general rise in prices does not imply a general rise in values. Indeed, inflation can be described with the help of the concept of value: the value of money falls in relation to the value of commodities. Value is immediately determined by the relationship between supply and demand: when a commodity is in short supply, consumers will pay more to get it and its value will rise (this is the 'temporary or market value'). In the long term, value is determined by *cost of production* (this is the 'permanent or Natural Value') (*CW*, vol. III, p. 497). Mill told Austin that in his *Principles of Political Economy* he had followed Ricardo: 'I doubt if there will be a single opinion (on pure political economy)…which may not be exhibited as a corollary from his doctrines' (*CW*, vol. XIII, p. 731). But on this issue he did not follow his mentor. Ricardo, here very nearly a Marxist before Marx, thought that cost of production could largely be resolved into one factor: the natural value of a commodity was almost entirely determined by the quantity of labour required to produce it – he had a '93 per cent labour theory of value' (O'Brien, 1975, p. 86). This was Mill's view also as a young man (*CW*, vol. XXII, p. 53), but by the time of his textbook he maintained that 'Cost of Production consists of…the wages of labour, and the profits of capital' (plus a few occasional elements besides) (*CW*, vol. III, p. 498).

Mill was at one with other classical economists in extolling competition and economic freedom. Competition promotes efficiency and nearly always benefits consumers by lowering prices. But he was not a dogmatic and unqualified advocate of free enterprise like nineteenth-century popularizers and liberal politicians such as Harriet Martineau, Richard Cobden or Robert Lowe. He was prepared to admit that temporary tariffs might be justifiable in young countries to protect new industries (*CW*, vol. XVI, p. 1043). He did not think that the free market invariably produces the greatest good – there are cases of systematic 'market failure' where state intervention is desirable. Though competition *between* firms was normally beneficial, he was not convinced that competition *inside* the firm – between employers and workers and between workers in sharing the gains – would always be appropriate, as we shall see in a later chapter.

Mill famously drew a distinction between the unchanging laws of production, and the variable laws of distribution, thereby opening a space in the classical framework for the consideration of socialism. Distribution must wait for a later chapter: the laws of production, the conditions under which humanity must produce wealth whether they like it or not, are considered here.

First, *production is proportional to capital* (*CW*, vol. II, p. 199). There are two sorts of capital, *fixed* and *circulating*. Fixed capital, relatively durable, takes the form for example of buildings, machinery and tools. Circulating capital pays for the recurrent costs – for raw materials, and the wages of labour. The classical economists tend to write as if the most important volume of capital is the volume used to pay wages, and in this way their theory has a slightly pre-industrial flavour. Any production task taking more than a day or so would be impossible without this capital. If capital did not advance wages to labourers, they would be unable to buy food and other necessaries in the interval between commencing the job and selling the finished product. The amount of productive activity which can go on and therefore the amount of wealth produced depends on the amount of capital saved up to pay wages. This saving or accumulation is only possible because capitalists abstain from consumption, deny themselves spending so as to have money left to set labourers to work. They will not do this without an incentive; interest on capital is that incentive, a *reward for abstinence*. *Profit*, received for example by a factory owner, consists of interest plus 'wages of superintendance' – a payment for the capitalist's labour in running the factory, plus any further sum required to compensate the capitalist if the business is risky.

Earlier economists worried that there would not be enough capital to set all labourers to work. Some, such as Ricardo, thought that mechanization created a special problem here. Machines could replace men, making it possible to produce more goods with less labour. If a capitalist took a portion of his circulating capital, which hitherto he had paid out in wages, and used it to buy a machine, that is to say changed it into fixed capital, he might be able to produce as much cloth as before, at a higher profit; but he would hire less labour. If such conversions happened on a large enough scale, then employment opportunities would contract and wages fall. Mill agreed that such things could happen; the highland clearances of the early nineteenth century were a striking example. The landowners invested their capital in fences and sheep, getting a higher income in return; but the rural poor were no longer required, and were forced to leave the land. But in the short and medium term at least, Mill was not much concerned about this, being more optimistic than his mentors. He had faith in the stupendous power of capital to accumulate. In a progressive economy like Britain's, the rate of saving was so high that new capital would rapidly flow in to make good any deficiency. He based his optimism in part upon the experience of the railway mania of the 1830s and 1840s, which had witnessed an unprecedented creation of fixed capital in the form of the railway network and its ancillaries; yet he believed this had not depressed employment and wages in other sectors of the economy.

Adam Smith had worried that if the government spent too much and therefore taxed too much, there would not be enough capital accumulation. This was expressed in terms of a distinction between *productive* and *unproductive spending*. Money spent hiring labourers was productive, because it created wealth; luxury spending or government spending merely destroyed wealth and was unproductive.

Second, Mill incorporates this in a further ineluctable law; '*Whether they like it or not, the unproductive expenditure of individuals will pro tanto tend to impoverish the community, and only their productive expenditure will enrich it*' (*CW*, vol. II, p. 199). But he is less worried about this too (*CW*, vol. II, p. 54) and insists that much government expenditure in fact *aids* production. Just as money spent on hedging and ditching increases the crop by protecting it, so government activity in protecting property and industry adds to the wealth of the nation (*CW*, vol. V, p. 282). He does not have the visceral hatred of taxation and government of some advocates of *laissez-faire*.

Third, *production is proportional to the efficiency of labour* (*CW*, vol. II, p. 199), for example to its energy, skill, and possession of advanced tools and machinery. An extended co-operation or combination of labour also enhances output; if the productive task is shared among several workers on a production line, there will be efficiency gains. A principal factor is that the combination of labour enables each worker to concentrate on that part of the productive task which he or she does best. Therefore there are economies of scale; a larger factory can have a more elaborate division of labour and greater output per worker. Combination of labour is also beneficial on an international scale. If Britain can produce woollen cloth more cheaply than Germany, and Germany can produce linen more cheaply than Britain, then both countries will obtain their requirements at less cost if Britain produces the woollen cloth and Germany the linen for both. What is saved can be spent producing something else, and so there will be more commodities to go round. This is a key component of the argument for free trade. If governments, by bounties or tariffs, encourage the production at home of what could be bought more cheaply abroad, the result will be that the nation and the mass of the people will be poorer.

Fourth, *the law of diminishing returns in agriculture*: 'Whether they like it or not, a double quantity of labour will not raise, on the same land, a double quantity of food, unless some improvement takes place in the processes of cultivation' (*CW*, vol. II, p. 199). Doubling the labour put into a given field – digging, manuring, watering and weeding it more thoroughly – will not double its yield. Nor in old, well-populated countries, will doubled labour double the food if it is used to bring new land into cultivation, for the best land will be under the plough already and the new land will consist of inferior soils. This is the form in which Mill chooses to state his adherence to Malthus's theory of population. In old countries there is a tendency for growth in population not to be matched by growth in food output, and therefore for the living standards of the mass to fall. A rapid increase in population could lead to poverty, famine and death. Malthus's doctrine was originally presented (in 1798) as a riposte to the utopias of Condorcet and Godwin: given that men and women *will* have sex and increase their numbers, poverty is the inevitable lot of the masses and utopia is impossible. Malthus's doctrine turned classical political economy from the generally optimistic stance of Adam Smith's *Wealth of Nations* of 1776 to a pervasive pessimism, helping to secure its reputation as the 'dismal science', as Carlyle called it. Both Malthus and Ricardo were inclined to think that public policies of poor relief were a mistake: if the poor were assured of food, they would breed recklessly and thereby make poverty more pervasive.

Another way of expressing the doctrine is in terms of the theory of a *wages fund*. As already explained, the classical economists thought that there was an accumulated sum of circulating capital available to pay wages: this was the wages fund. We might think of that fund, not as money but as the 'wage goods' money will buy, principally food, in order to sustain workers and their families. If population grows faster than the wages fund, faster than the ever-renewing stock of food, that fund and that food will have to be shared between more hands and more mouths, which on average will get less to eat.

Mill was always a neo-Malthusian, but he unpacked the consequences of Malthus's doctrine in a kindlier and more optimistic manner. Basically he did this by making a very simple move, turning Malthus on his head as it were. Malthus in 1798 argued that because population tends to grow faster than the food supply, therefore the living standard of the people tends to fall. Mill argued that if the people can limit their population growth to a level lower than the growth in food output, then their standard of living will rise. Here is the solution to the problem of poverty. To put it another way, if the labouring classes can control their numbers then, instead of them competing for food, food in the form of the wages fund (that is to say of capital seeking investment) will compete for them and they will be able to bargain for higher wages. Mill was presenting this argument as early as 1823, advocating artificial contraception as the way to do it (*CW*, vol. XXII, pp. 82–4). After being arrested for this advocacy, Mill, nothing daunted, put his faith in sexual restraint, which he suggested would be more likely if labourers became better educated.

There were less pessimistic hints in Malthus and Ricardo themselves, which Mill adopted. They thought, for example, that Nemesis could be delayed, perhaps for a long time, by importing food from developing countries where population was not pressing hard on the land, or by exporting population, encouraging emigration, to such countries. This was why the classical economists were so hostile to the Corn Laws, which discouraged the importation of cheap foreign grain. Malthus's first edition had been uncompromising; with grim relish he insisted that the poor would inevitably descend to a bare subsistence. In later editions he recognized that there was a *customary* standard of living for working people, which might well include certain expected comforts and even luxuries beyond mere subsistence. They might restrain their breeding, above all by delaying marriage, in order to maintain this customary standard.

Mill thought that the state had responsibility for the poor, and should provide poor relief. Convicted criminals are fed in prison: it would be absurd and unjust to leave law-abiding paupers to starve. The poor would hate the rich if there were no poor relief (*CW*, vol. XV, p. 897). But it should not encourage population growth, and therefore he supported the New Poor Law of 1834, whose architect was the economist Nassau Senior. The central principle of that law was the principle of less eligibility and therefore the banning of outdoor relief (that is, relief in their own homes). The lot of the pauper should be less eligible than that of the poorest person in employment. The way to achieve this was to give relief only in the workhouse, where conditions could be calculated for unpleasantness: monotonous diet, confinement, separation of men, women and children, drudging work. The poor would wish to avoid this, and therefore would be motivated to seek work and restrict the size of their families. This, Mill thought, had been the principle of the Elizabethan poor law, and as long as it was rigidly enforced, it worked. But towards the end of the eighteenth century, relaxation crept in, the poor were relieved without being required to enter a workhouse (indoor relief), and as a result population burgeoned, making the measures of 1834 necessary (*CW*, vol. XXIV, p. 1006). Today, historians regard the New Poor Law and its workhouses with distaste; it was inhuman, and unnecessarily so, for the evidence does not support the conclusion that outdoor relief stimulated population while indoor relief restrained it. But Mill, preoccupied as he was with the population problem, advocated the workhouse system throughout his life.

Mill had another solution to the problem of population: he was an enthusiast for peasant proprietorship. Mill believed that a peasant, owning his own plot of land, had the greatest incentive to work and save, for all the rewards would accrue to himself and his family. This would only be so if the holding were large enough to provide a decent standard of living; a peasant whose plot was too small would be without hope and therefore without a motive for providence. The peasant proprietor knew how many mouths his land would feed, and exercised restraint so that he, and his children after him, could continue to live in comfort. Mill painted a radiant picture of the simple comfort, respectability and happiness of such families, and this was not utopian pipe-dreaming: he had solid evidence to back up his claims, evidence which reveals him as the European man he was. Mill had read about and witnessed peasant societies, in Italy, France and the Low Countries.

Mill did not agree with other economists that large-scale English capitalist farming was the key to efficiency and progress. Some large farms, with wealthy capitalist farmers, are desirable, because they have the resources to lead the way with experiments and innovations; but in general smallholdings are better. Full ownership by the peasant is ideal, but some of the benefits can be gained with other modes of tenure. What is vital is very long leases at fixed rents so that the peasant knows he will enjoy the improvements won by his labour. He quotes 'Give a man the secure possession of a bleak rock, and he will turn it into a garden; give him a nine years' lease of a garden, and he will convert it into a desert' (*CW*, vol. II, p. 274). By the late 1850s the censuses revealed that the threat of imminent over-population in Britain was receding. Thanks to technical progress in agriculture, food prices were falling; wages were rising. Mill began to shift his emphasis when considering population from economic to environmental and moral considerations: excessive numbers of children were degrading for women (*CW*, vol. XIV, pp. 88–9).

From the laws of production, we turn to Mill's account of how wealth is distributed in a capitalist society. In the domain of pure theory Mill follows Ricardo closely. First, there is *an inverse relation of profits and wages*. A factory earns a given amount of wealth: if more is given to the hands there will be less for the master and vice versa. Second, as already mentioned, there is a *wages fund*, a given volume of circulating capital destined to set hands to work and pay their wages. It follows that if a particular group of workers, by strike action, gets a bigger share of the wages fund, then it is likely that other workers will get less. This casts doubt on the ability of trade unions to secure gains for the working class as a whole, but Mill and the other classical economists never doubted that workers should be free to form unions and conduct strikes. At the very least, their failure to secure real gains would teach them the important economic lesson that the only way forward was by restraining population. Mill's evolving attitude to the wages fund theory merits further consideration later. The remaining form of income, rent, arises from the difference between good and inferior land. When population is high, demand for food and therefore the price of food are high, and a farmer can earn a living by farming low-yielding soil. A farmer on soil which is more fertile or more favourably situated will produce his living plus a surplus which he pays to a landlord as rent.

We can now understand Mill's theory of the likely evolution of the capitalist economy towards a *stationary state*. If population grows, and recourse is had to poorer soils in order to grow the food required, the difference between the best and worst land under cultivation will increase and rents will increase accordingly. Population growth, therefore, automatically benefits the landlord while he sleeps, without any effort on his part. But in the long run it does not benefit labourers or capitalists. As food prices rise, labourers have less to spend on other commodities and eventually can afford less food. But there is a limit to this declension. When wages fall too low, workers and their families become under-nourished; premature death slows the rate of population increase. This shifts the balance of supply and demand in the labour market in favour of the labourers, and wages begin to rise. In this way, wages will continually be fluctuating round about the level of subsistence. As long as population continues to grow, the cost of subsistence and therefore the cost of wages will increase. But, as we saw earlier, a rise in wages has as a necessary consequence a fall in profits. If profits fall too low the motive to save and invest will be weakened and capital will cease to accumulate. Growth will stop: this is the *stationary state* as envisaged by Ricardo, a dismal condition with the masses on the verge of subsistence.

But Mill, as we have seen, hoped that workers would control their breeding to secure a high standard of living. Still, the stationary state would come in the end. Given the rapid accumulation of capital demonstrated by recent experience, if the people restrained their numbers, capital and therefore jobs would increase faster than workers seeking employment. In a sellers' market labour would be able to demand high wages, the rate of profit would fall (*CW*, vol. V, p. 300) and would continue to fall as the imbalance increased. Mill thought that Britain was already within a handsbreadth of the stationary state; the basic return on capital was just 3 per cent and if it fell below 1 per cent there would be no incentive to abstain and save.

There were factors delaying the onset of the stationary state. Britain was exporting surplus capital overseas, to developing countries with smaller stocks of capital and a lower rate of saving. Commercial crises, crashes and slumps destroyed quantities of capital when firms went bankrupt, leaving room for fresh accumulation in the upturn. But this is not the main point. What principally distinguishes Mill from earlier economists is that he thought the stationary state would be no bad thing, if it was combined with a high working-class standard of living. He did not think that the pursuit of ever more wealth and ever more consumption was the proper goal of human existence:

> I confess I am not charmed with the ideal of life held out by those who think that the normal state of human beings is that of struggling to get on; that the trampling, crushing, elbowing, and treading on each other's heels ... are the most desirable lot of human kind (*CW*, vol. III, p. 754).

Furthermore the prospect of an over-exploited, over-peopled world, the inevitable result of unending economic growth, had no appeal for him (*CW*, vol. III, pp. 756).

What is Mill's place in the history of economic thought? In his Preface he claims to have written a book 'similar in its object and general conception to that of Adam Smith' and 'different from ... any treatise on Political Economy ... in England since the work of Adam Smith' (*CW*, vol. II, pp. xci–xcii). He means that he has not written a book of pure, abstract theory; the *Principles of Political Economy* contains a wealth of detailed information, and extended discussions of practical implications and economic policies which we must consider in a later chapter. As we have seen, Mill insists that the economic theory is Ricardian. Without doubt Mill theorizes within Ricardo's framework and is therefore a central classical political economist, but his differences from

Ricardo should not be under-estimated. We have seen how he transformed the 'dismal science' into something more optimistic. His insistence that, while the laws of production are ineluctable, distribution is a matter of choice, differs sharply from Ricardo (O'Brien, 1975, p. 46). Although his detailed technical contributions have not been considered in this chapter, it is important to note that he was one of 'a tiny handful of enormously fertile theoretical innovators in the history of economics' (Stigler, 1976, p. 66) who made important original contributions to, for example, the theory of international trade – 'one of the greatest performances in the history of economics' (O'Brien, 1975, p. 183) – and to the theory of the trade cycle (*CW*, vol. V, pp. ix–x).

Mill's originality is played down in Hollander's two-volume study, apparently because of Hollander's scholastic ambition to argue that all the great economists agreed with each other (Coats, 1987, pp. 311–12, 314). In particular, he denies that Mill rescued economics from the 'Ricardian Vice'. Ricardo and James Mill have been judged excessively abstract theoreticians, whose doctrines fit together with admirable logic precisely because they rest upon simplified assumptions which relate only imperfectly to the real world. As Brougham put it in the House of Commons, Ricardo made his case for the repeal of the Corn Laws as if he had 'descended from some other planet'. Joseph Schumpeter in his *History of Economic Analysis* referred to the habit of drawing policy conclusions from abstract models as the 'Ricardian Vice'. Hollander denies that Ricardo was guilty of such a vice, and therefore also denies that John Stuart Mill's economics marked a new departure. Most historians of economics have agreed with Schumpeter rather than Hollander (O'Brien, 1975, pp. 3–4), and Mill's avowed return to Adam Smith can be interpreted in this way. In a letter of 1830 to the French economist J.B. Say, Mill admits that his mentors were too abstract, and associates himself with a rising generation of economists more sensitive to complicating factors and historical diversity (*CW*, vol. XXXII, p. 10). But he was loyal to Ricardo, and normally attributed the 'Ricardian Vice' to others, such as the MP Robert Lowe (*CW*, vol. XXVIII, pp. 255–6; vol. V, p. 671).

Classical political economy, and Mill's textbook, reigned supreme until the last decades of the nineteenth century; after 1870 it gradually succumbed to the 'marginalist revolution' and the triumph of 'Neoclassicism', associated with Jevons and Marshall in England. Neoclassicism was more purely scientific than classical political economy and in general more mathematical, with the result that the ordinary man or woman who could read and understand Mill was now excluded from serious economic debate. Whereas classical political economy focussed upon macroeconomic questions of growth and income distribution, Neoclassicism moved the microeconomic question of price determination to centre stage. It dispensed with key classical ideas, such as 'natural value' as distinguished from market price, and the distinction between productive and unproductive spending. In his last years Mill knew of, but chose to reject, some of these new developments (*CW*, vol. XVII, p. 1862). But much of Mill's thought was simply incorporated into the new paradigm, and his reflections on economic policy, to be considered in a later chapter, continue to be significant and relevant.

4

UTILITARIANISM AND LIBERTY

The Essays and their Reputation

In his essay *Utilitarianism*, Mill writes that 'The creed which accepts as the foundation of morals, Utility, or the Greatest Happiness Principle, holds that actions are right in proportion as they tend to promote happiness, wrong as they tend to produce the reverse of happiness' (*CW*, vol. X, p. 210). By itself this formulation could have come from the pen of Utilitarianism's founding father, Jeremy Bentham. We may unpack Bentham's classic Utilitarianism into three central ideas. First, actions are judged right or wrong with reference to their consequences; Utilitarianism is a *consequentialist* moral theory. Actions are right if they produce *good* consequences, wrong if they produce *bad* ones. Second, *good* and *bad* ultimately mean *happiness* and *unhappiness*. Bentham's Utilitarianism therefore is a form of *hedonism*. Third, in judging actions or types of actions, we are invited to add up the sum of happiness produced and the sum of unhappiness, and to compare the sums. The rightness is determined by the surplus of happiness over unhappiness. Utilitarianism, then, is an *aggregative* moral theory.

Consequentialism, hedonism and aggregation: all three central ideas are contentious and create difficulties. Consequentialism runs up against the belief, held by ordinary persons and by some philosophers, that certain actions are intrinsically wrong, regardless of their good consequences, such as telling a lie so as not to hurt someone's feelings, or helping a terminally ill person to die so as to relieve them of pain. The charge against hedonism was made by critics such as Coleridge and Carlyle, who contended that Utilitarianism was a philosophy for pigs. Their high-minded disdain for sensual pleasure might not have

79

much resonance today, but still they have a point. Surely there are ultimate goods other than happiness. After all, didn't Mill himself write a
passionate defence of liberty, thereby proposing that liberty is an ultimate good? As for aggregation, that would appear to permit the sacrifice of the one or the few for the sake of the many – Iphigeneia so that
the Greeks might have a prosperous voyage to Troy, Myra Hindley to
appease the British public – but doesn't justice forbid us to do such
things? Furthermore, aggregation appears to imply an intolerable
moral tyranny. If it is my duty in every action of my life to produce the
greatest possible surplus of pleasure over pain, then I will have to
spend a great deal of time calculating which is the best action. And the
result of my calculations will often require me to sacrifice my own pleasures for the sake of the greater good, never buying a silk tie or a bottle
of claret if I might instead give money to Oxfam.

As well as real difficulties, there were bogus ones. In the first half of
the century, critics had mauled Utilitarianism, caricaturing Bentham's
philosophy and giving it a bad reputation, as Mill was well aware (*CW*,
vol. XV, p. 745). Coleridge, fastening upon the emphasis on pleasure,
contended that it was a philosophy of selfishness. There was a grain of
truth in this charge, in that Bentham and James Mill subscribed to a
largely Hobbesian theory of selfish motivation: but essentially it was
false, because Utilitarianism prescribes not the agent's happiness but
the happiness of all concerned. Then there is the assimilation, implied
by Dickens in *Hard Times* for example, of Utilitarianism as a moral philosophy to Utilitarianism as the narrow, philistine pursuit of material
gain and heartless efficiency – the unacceptable face of the industrial
revolution. Mill himself was far removed from Mr Gradgrind in that
novel. He had a Coleridgean disdain for the pure commercial spirit
(*CW*, vol. XII, p. 31) and criticized the English and Americans for mea-
suring 'the merit of all things by their tendency to increase the number
of steam engines, and to make human beings as good machines and
therefore as mere machines as those' (*CW*, vol. XIII, p. 622). After his
mental crisis he was a consistent opponent of mere 'utilitarian', professional education, preferring a broad curriculum designed to turn out
wise and cultivated individuals (*CW*, vol. XXXII, pp. 21, 186).

Mill's essay on Utilitarianism succeeded in transforming it from a
detested object of attack to an account of morality to be discussed seriously and sympathetically by both professional philosophers and the
educated public (Schneewind, 1976, pp. 49–52). He easily disposed of
the crude misconceptions, and his response to the real difficulties was

to propose a very sophisticated and subtle version of Utilitarianism. The result is much richer than, and in some ways quite different from, the moral philosophy of his father and of Jeremy Bentham. Mill does not definitively resolve all the issues, as we shall see; but his moral theory is a real contender, even today.

Turning now to Mill's other great essay, the best-known passage of the *Liberty* asserts 'one very simple principle' (*CW*, vol. XVIII, pp. 223–4) which proposes Mill's celebrated distinction between 'self-regarding actions' (which when performed intentionally may not be interfered with under any circumstances) and 'other-regarding actions' (which under certain circumstances may be prevented). The principle does not apply to children who must often be protected against themselves, nor to backward peoples, barbarians, for the same reason. The passage also makes it clear that Mill is worried about two modes of interference with individual liberty. The first and obvious one is interference by the state, by means of laws and penalties. Mill fears that democracy may make this worse; a tyranny of the majority may develop, which will use the power of the state to crush nonconforming minorities (*CW*, vol. XVIII, p. 219). The other mode of interference is the pressure of public opinion, the disapproval of society, the attempt to make everyone conform. Mill tells us that in England, in some senses a free country, interference by the state is less than elsewhere. But the pressure of public opinion is heavier (*CW*, vol. XVIII, pp. 222–3). He worried that the proliferation of popular newspapers provided a powerful organ through which this intolerance could be expressed (*CW*, vol. XVIII, pp. 268–9).

Macaulay thought that Mill was crying 'Fire!' in Noah's flood – liberty was in no danger in mid-nineteenth-century England. Macaulay may have felt there was too much liberty: by Mill's standards there was plainly not enough, and some commentators have judged that an illiberal persecuting spirit continued to flourish well into the twentieth century (Russell, 1969, p. 10; Annan, 1969, pp. 40–1). Many contemporary commentators profoundly disagreed with the book, and a recurrent criticism was that the liberty Mill advocated would undermine religion. They were perfectly right to focus on this: both the essay itself and Mill's correspondence confirm Mill's preoccupation with religious intolerance, which could still deny Roman Catholic widows custody of their children, exclude professed unbelievers from parliament and deny them justice in the courts. He must also have been motivated by the social disapproval he experienced on account of his twenty-year friendship with a married woman.

The simple principle, so memorably formulated, raises many difficulties; three of the most important will be highlighted here. First, as
Himmelfarb has argued, liberty is a complex matter; how can one simple principle be an appropriate way of tackling it (Himmelfarb, 1974,
pp. 132–3, 168)? Is the principle *adequate*? Second, as critics have
pointed out from the very beginning, does it make sense to distinguish
between self- and other-regarding actions? Unless I am an unobtrusive
tramp with no friends and relations, then most of the things I do have
the potential to affect or concern others: if I swear, or get drunk, or eat
meat, or read the *Satanic Verses*, someone will be offended. The class of
actions which are purely self-regarding might be a very small class
indeed, and therefore Mill's principle may in practice do little or nothing for the cause of liberty. This second difficulty concerns the *meaning*
of the principle. Third, is Mill's defence of liberty *consistent* with his
Utilitarianism? This is an obvious difficulty, because Mill has said that
'His own good, either physical or moral, is not a sufficient warrant'
(for interference). We may not interfere with an individual's liberty
as defined by the principle even for his own good; apparently this is a
repudiation of consequentialism.

Mill can be defended against these criticisms of the adequacy, meaning and consistency of his principle of liberty, as we shall see. Part of
the defence involves a recognition that the principle is not as simple as
he claims. To understand it fully we have to read the two essays *On
Liberty* and *Utilitarianism* together, and draw light from other writings.
Since the work of Rees, Ryan, Lyons, Berger, Gray and others, it will not
do to dismiss Mill (as earlier critics often did) by analysing brief passages hacked out of context. But, on the other hand, we ought not to
make Mill more consistent and defensible than he actually was. Have
recent commentators 'improved' or rewritten Mill, thereby to an extent
losing sight of the nineteenth-century philosopher in nineteenth-
century context? A certain amount of careful and sensitive 'improving'
is probably legitimate. Mill wrote before the expansion and profession-
alization of academic philosophy in this century. That professionaliza-
tion produced standards of precise and technical formulation which
Mill did not meet because he was not trying to meet them and because
they had not yet been established. It can therefore be argued that it is
legitimate to reformulate Mill's moral and political philosophy with the
precision he would have employed had he been writing today with an
eye to captious critics, always provided that we do not change his
meaning in the process.

Mill's Theory of Right and Wrong Actions

Let us begin with his account of duty. Mill's sophisticated version of Utilitarianism does not insist that it is always our duty to act so as to procure the most happiness, immediately and directly. For, first, he had learnt from Carlyle that the direct pursuit of happiness as an end in itself leads to disappointment, and that 'those only are happy...who have their minds fixed on some other object than their own happiness; on the happiness of others, on the improvement of mankind, even on some art or pursuit, followed not as a means, but as itself an ideal end' (*CW*, vol. 1, pp. 145–7).

On the face of it, this looks like an abandonment of classic Utilitarianism – Mill here recommends other ideal ends than happiness. Later in this chapter we shall see that no abandonment has occurred; but, for the time being, the thesis has been proposed that it is not necessary always to have our sights firmly fixed on happiness. One might make the further point that while it is difficult to make people happy, because happiness is so elusive, suffering is much more concrete, often with obvious causes (crime, poverty, unemployment, lack of liberty) and that therefore, as both Bentham and Mill thought, our first aim should be the 'negative utilitarian' one of alleviating misery (Bentham, 1967, p. 281; *CW*, vol. X, p. 216; Walker, 1974, pp. 424–5).

Second, Mill's Utilitarianism, and Bentham's too, insists that we pay attention to the long-term as well as the short-term consequences of our actions. Seizing the money of a rich man and distributing it among fifty poor ones might look utilitarian – their fifty lots of happiness might outweigh his solitary misery – but taking a longer view, the consequence might be to make all property owners, large and small, feel insecure in their possession, with dire economic consequences and a disastrous increase in the unhappiness of the community. Bentham and Mill insist that security is a vital condition of happiness and this is one reason why our behaviour, much of the time, should be governed, not by calculations of pleasure and pain for each action, but rather by rules of conduct which experience has proved to have generally good consequences. A rule-governed society is one where we know what to expect and therefore feel secure. Another reason for rules is that they save us the time and trouble of calculating the consequences each time before we act, thereby enabling us to act more quickly (*CW*, vol. X, pp. 224–5). A third reason is that, while there is a margin of uncertainty about the consequences of a particular act (telling a lie, for instance, which in a specific instance might do more good than harm), the consequences of classes of acts are more predictable (a general practice of lying would definitely be harmful – *CW*, vol. X, pp. 180–3). This is not to say, in accordance with twentieth-century philosophical terminology, that Mill is a 'rule Utilitarian' who thinks that the principle of utility is *only* to be used to assess rules of conduct, as opposed to an 'act Utilitarian' who proposes to use it to assess particular actions. Rather, Mill is a 99 per cent *indirect* Utilitarian who thinks that most of the time we apply the principle of utility indirectly by following rules and that only rarely do we need to calculate the consequences of a specific act (primarily when two rules conflict) (*CW*, vol. X, p. 226; Lyons, 1994, p. 17; Hampsher-Monk, 1992, pp. 363–7).

So far, Mill has not departed in essence from classic Utilitarianism: we now come to a place where he does, with much trumpeting. In his essay on *Bentham* he accuses his mentor of excessive moralism. Bentham heaps praise or blame on every action and every character solely in accordance with the criterion of utilitarian morality. Mill argues (not entirely clearly – Ryan, 1974, p. 106) that actions and character traits are also to be evaluated by non-moral criteria: they may be beautiful or loveable rather than right or wrong (*CW*, vol. X, pp. 112–13). Mill develops this somewhat differently in his *Logic*. There he proposes an Art of Life having three departments: Morality, which is concerned with the Right; Prudence or Policy, whose business is with the Expedient; and Aesthetics, dealing with 'the Beautiful or Noble, in human conduct and works' (*CW*, vol. VIII, p. 949). All three departments are grounded ultimately on utility: morality, efficiency and aesthetic considerations have value because they promote happiness. Nevertheless what this implies is that whole areas of human conduct and character are not subject to direct *moral* evaluation at all, but are to be judged instead on criteria of efficiency, beauty and nobility. Morality occupies only a part of the field of utility, sharing it with aesthetics and prudence. Mill's Utilitarianism therefore is by no means an all-embracing moral tyranny.

This is further evidenced by Mill's *Auguste Comte and Positivism* of 1865. He criticizes Comte for being 'a morality-intoxicated man. Every question with him is one of morality, and no motive but that of morality is permitted'. Comte maintains that there can be no distinction between an ordinarily moral person who simply does the minimum that duty requires, and a moral hero who does the maximum, performing acts of 'supererogation' which go beyond the call of duty. For it is the duty of all of us to do the maximum, to devote all our time and energies to the common good: it is immoral to do less than this. Mill thinks that more happiness will result in the end if we spend most of our time pursuing our own goals, and therefore he leaves, and insists upon, a space for acts of supererogation (*CW*, vol. X, pp. 336–7). Mill's Utilitarianism contracts the domain of morality so that most acts are neither right nor wrong, but rather indifferent, permissible.

So how are we to distinguish between acts which are subject to moral praise or blame, and those which are not? The theory of this is explained in the essay on Comte and in the last chapter of *Utilitarianism*. Mill argues that there is an intrinsic connection between morality and punishment, an idea he may have learnt from Austin's lectures on jurisprudence which he attended in 1829. When we say that an act is morally blameable, we are also saying that it would be appropriate to discourage it by means of a *sanction* or *punishment*. By this Mill does not simply mean a prison sentence or a fine. Punishment can take other forms. As well as legal punishment there is what Bentham calls the *moral or popular sanction*, that is to say the informal punishment which stems from the disapproval of others. Mill adds a further sanction, proclaiming in his essay on *Bentham* that the master failed to observe it: namely the punishment of one's own disapproving conscience in the form of guilt and remorse. An action falls into the province of morality therefore, only if it is appropriate to punish it in one of these three ways. Whether a sanction is appropriate, and which sanction in any particular case, is determined with reference to utility. Punishment directly and immediately causes unhappiness. Only if punishing an action will promote more happiness than it causes unhappiness should it be regarded as an action within the domain of morality.

Some examples will make this clear. The general happiness emphatically requires that acts of murder shall not be committed. It is therefore in accordance with utility that the severest legal punishment shall be attached to the rule 'Thou shalt not kill'. Truthfulness promotes happiness by making society work better, but there would be a net loss of happiness if every liar were imprisoned. It is therefore appropriate to punish lying informally, showing liars that we neither like nor trust them, and that we will not give them our help and support. The general happiness also requires that citizens should be ready to give in order to help those in need. But it would not be in accordance with utility to punish people for not being charitable. The appropriate sanction is the approval and disapproval of one's own conscience, and so it is desirable to educate children and form public opinion in order to give citizens charitable consciences. Happiness will also be increased by nobility of character, but little would be gained by causing slobs to feel unhappy. Therefore the recommendation, 'Be noble', comes without a sanction attached to it, and hence is not a moral recommendation at all.

In the light of these distinctions we can understand Mill's explanation of justice. Mill acknowledges that justice is very important to us; we care about it deeply. Perceived injustices – when someone is deprived of what is rightfully theirs, or is wrongly imprisoned, or is the victim of a breach of promise – raise up in us a peculiarly strong sense of moral indignation. We seem to care more about justice than we do about utility. We would not wish an innocent person to be imprisoned, even though their imprisonment produced the public good. Does this mean that the morality of justice is different from the morality of utility, more fundamental and important perhaps? Mill insists this is not so. The principles of justice carry the moral weight they do precisely because their observance is conducive to utility. We feel strongly about justice, because injustice is desperately anti-utilitarian. But for most of the time we do not make the connection between justice and utility, because the principles of justice are so familiar to us. The human race has got into the habit of desiring justice for its own sake, and has lost sight of the connection between justice and utility.

Unjust acts arouse our special indignation; we always feel that they should be punished, if not by the state then by public opinion. *Justice*, Mill explains, corresponds to *right*. Justice is owed, not like benevolence to humanity in general, but to assignable persons. An act of injustice violates a specific person's specific right. Rights are enforced by laws and moral rules which are of the most fundamental importance to well being and happiness. These laws and rules protect individuals against harm, and in the exercise of their liberty; they protect them in the enjoyment of those things to which they have a right, for example by promise, contract, labour and inheritance. I have a right not to be harmed, a right to be free, a right to demand that others keep their promises to me, a right to my property and to the fruits of my labour. Violations of my rights are injustice, and ought to be punished. The idea of justice has unique moral force, because justice protects security: 'Nearly all other earthly benefits are needed by one person, not needed by another; and many of them can, if necessary, be cheerfully foregone, or replaced by something else; but security no human being can possibly do without' (*CW*, vol. X, p. 251).

Mill's Theory of the Good

For Mill 'good' means pleasure or happiness; but what he understands by those terms is an especially difficult topic, and a definitive interpretation is not possible. Either Mill's thinking or his expression of it is not perfectly clear, and therefore there has been considerable debate about his meaning.

It is traditional in discussing this to contrast Mill's 'modified hedonism' with Bentham's 'simple hedonism', a contrast caught in Mill's distinction between higher and lower pleasures. Bentham too recognized that pleasures differ in quality (Hoag, 1992, p. 249), but has a notorious reputation as the philosopher who thought that 'Pushpin is as good as poetry'. Mill played his part in creating an image of Bentham as a crude hedonist, arguing that the older man's account of happiness was fundamentally defective. For example, according to Mill, Bentham failed to recognize that humans can find their happiness not only in the enjoyment of simple pleasures but also in the pursuit of spiritual perfection, when they set up a standard of personal excellence and try to live up to it (*CW*, vol. X, p. 95). Mill depicts the older Utilitarianism as thinking of human beings as passive consumers of pleasures.

If these accusations are justified, Bentham is open to the charge that his form of hedonism would be compatible with a condition in which euphoria was achieved by means of drugs as in Huxley's *Brave New World*, or, in Nozick's science-fiction example, by connecting people to pleasure machines. Mill rules these twentieth-century fantasies out in 1832:

> If the multifarious labours of [humanity] were performed for us by supernatural agency, and there were no demand for either wisdom or virtue, but barely for stretching out our hands and enjoying, small would be our enjoyment, for there would be nothing which man could any longer prize in man (*CW*, vol. I, p. 330).

His best-known statement of a modified hedonism is contained in his essay *Utilitarianism*, where he maintains that no developed human being would wish for an animal existence which failed to deploy the higher faculties (*CW*, vol. X, p. 211). Putting the essays on *Bentham* and *Utilitarianism* together it appears that the higher faculties include intellect, and the active capacities associated with power, freedom and creativity.

It is a conception of happiness which lays stress upon sociability, but also upon pride, personal independence and excitement. Finally it idealizes dignity, thereby alluding to that department of the aesthetic, of the noble, which Mill identified when outlining the Art of Life in his *Logic*. Mill's repudiation of passive hedonism is clearest in his insistence that happiness is not the same thing as satisfaction or contentment; a contented fool is less happy than a wise man whose faculties are all at a stretch, even if the wise man is not contented. Mill concludes by saying that 'It is better to be a human being dissatisfied than a pig satisfied; better to be Socrates dissatisfied than a fool satisfied' (*CW*, vol. X, p. 212).

Mill does not advocate complete abstinence from the 'lower', sensual pleasures; in his diary he wrote that the modern world needed Epicurean enjoyment rather than Stoic or Puritan self-denial (*CW*, vol. XXVI, p. 666). Still, there remains a suspicion that he under-rated simple enjoyments, especially sexual ones. The ideal life will be 'made up of few and transitory pains, many and various pleasures, with a decided predominance of the active over the passive' (*CW*, vol. X, p. 215). How do we know that one pleasure is of a higher quality than another? The only way is to consult those who have experienced both. This sounds élitist, awakening the suspicion that the arbiters are those who like reading philosophy and listening to chamber music, rather than those whose idea of a good day out centres upon football, beer and a vindaloo with friends. This is unfair to Mill; given his stress upon activity, 'passively hearing Mozart or Beethoven may be less valuable than critically listening to "heavy metal"...or Appalachian folk tunes' (Hoag, 1992, p. 276). Also, it cannot be doubted that he would like *everybody* to be educated enough to enjoy Plato and string quartets.

It has been said that to distinguish higher and lower pleasures logically implies the abandonment of hedonism and therefore classic Utilitarianism (Bradley, 1927, p. 119). To prefer one pleasure to another on grounds of *quantity* – for example because it lasts longer – is consistent with maintaining that only pleasure is good. But to prefer it on grounds of *quality*, because it is *better*, implies some other criterion – for example, beauty or dignity – for distinguishing between pleasures. Therefore Mill is no longer saying that only pleasure is good: he must be invoking some other independent good. This criticism is clearly mistaken, as can be shown by the assessment of wine. Drinking wine is a pleasure, variable in terms of quantity: two glasses are more pleasurable than one. The pleasure also varies in terms of quality: good wine is more pleasurable to drink than ordinary wine. If asked to specify the characteristics making for a better-quality wine, the taster will mention bouquet, colour, complexity, length and so on. But this is not to say that something other than pleasure is good: the characteristics cited are ingredients of the pleasure of drinking wine. Therefore it is logically possible to maintain both that only pleasure is good, and also that pleasures differ in quality. But does Mill really stick to the classic Utilitarian doctrine that only pleasure is good? He recognizes that men and women apparently desire many things other than happiness, such as virtue, money, power and fame. They may be desired for their own sakes, and not merely as a means to happiness. He insists, however, that this does not contradict Utilitarianism; virtue, money, power, fame, etc. are desired as *parts* of happiness. They all bring pleasure.

This idea needs further explanation. Mill, as mentioned earlier, belongs to the tradition of associationist psychology. Associationists believe that many sensations – sights, sounds, smells, tastes, feels – come accompanied with perceptible pleasure or pain. Hence, certain things are naturally pleasurable. Other things, not originally pleasurable, come to be associated by habit with pleasure, as for example the sight of home may call up memories of the pleasures enjoyed within its walls. Mill distinguishes between *mechanical* and *chemical* associations. A mechanical association links two ideas together, but they remain distinct and separable. In a chemical association, the component ideas have become so intensely fused and united that they form an organic whole in the mind, constituting a single experience. This is what has happened in the case of things such as virtue which are desired for their own sake. Originally virtue was mechanically associated with pleasure, because the child was praised and rewarded for virtuous acts. He or she did not desire virtue for its own sake, but as a means to the reward/ pleasure. But over a long time and by frequent repetition, the ideas of virtue and pleasure became chemically compounded and inseparable. The idea of virtue became pleasant in and for itself, an intrinsic and essential part of the person's happiness.

In yet another way Mill departs from classic Utilitarianism. The latter, in saying that only pleasure or happiness are good as ends means this in the obvious, commonsense way: what is good are certain feelings in people's minds. Perhaps this is what Mill means most of the time; but not always. I think that Berger and Brink are right to draw attention to the fact that for Mill the happiness which people aim at as a goal or consequence of action can sometimes take the form of a state of affairs – being virtuous, or wise, or noble – which does not necessarily include pleasurable *feelings* (Berger, 1984, p. 14; Brink, 1992, pp. 69–70). Pleasurable feelings only come in as a *cause* of the action – the agent feels happy at the thought of attaining the goal. They are not proposed as a *consequence* of the action, and indeed may not be a consequence (*CW*, vol. X, p. 12). This is most convincingly implied by Mill's repeated remarks about the death of Lincoln by an assassin's bullet. Mill proposed that Lincoln's death as a martyr in the hour of triumph was an ultimate happiness for him, the crown of a noble life: and he cannot have meant that Lincoln *felt* happy in his death-agony, for he died 'almost unconsciously' (*CW*, vol. XVI, pp. 1044, 1051, 1057, 1063).

Is Mill's theory vulnerable at this point to the kind of criticism Macaulay levelled at James Mill? Only pleasure is good, that is to say, desirable as an end: has Mill, trying to defend this thesis against the charge of falsity, so expanded the meaning of 'pleasure' as to render it vacuous? If we approach his theory as a mere definition of 'good', this conclusion is hard to resist, and we are likely to agree with Skorupski that Mill would have been better advised to retain the consequentialism of classic Utilitarianism while giving up the hedonism, recognizing that there are other goods than pleasure or happiness such as autonomy (Skorupski, 1989, p. 283). But Mill is not primarily concerned with definition, nor with approaching the question as a twentieth-century philosopher would; however mistakenly he is providing a sketch of a scientific account of how an elaborate conception of the good evolves out of a simple psychological structure, remaining rooted in the fundamental human desire for pleasure and aversion to pain.

Has Mill reached the point of abandoning an objective and universal account of the good? Is he in effect saying that happiness varies from person to person; 'one man's meat is another man's poison'; what pleases in Beijing does not please in New York, and so on? If this is so, then Bentham's hedonism, which treats *pleasures* and *pains* as entities largely calculable in abstraction from historical circumstances, has been comprehensively abandoned. Utilitarianism will have turned into 'preference Utilitarianism' which seeks to satisfy people's preferences whatever they may be. In spite of having once written that 'there is nothing whatever which may not become an object of desire or of dislike by association', Mill was not a preference Utilitarian. The distinction between higher and lower pleasures, and the doctrine that competent persons can select the higher ones, not just from their own point of view but for everybody, rules this out. His position was a complex one, combining a belief in moral truth with a recognition of moral evolution. I do not agree with Gray that to all intents and purposes Mill repudiates a universal human essence (Gray & Smith, 1991, p. 205). Though he nowhere provides an extended exposition of a theory of human attributes, he commits himself to the belief that at a deep level human nature is universal and unchanging: 'man's nature changes not, though surrounding circumstances do' (*CW*, vol. XII, p. 101; Robson, 1976, pp. 143–60). The fundamental economy of pleasure and pain is the same for all. On that foundation, a variety of structures can be built – there is more than one pattern of human excellence – but not just *any* structure. Morality evolves and rules of conduct change 'from the progress of intelligence, from more authentic and enlarged experience, and from alterations in the condition of the human race' (*CW*, vol. X, p. 74). This is entirely to be welcomed, for human life would be poorer and less happy 'if there were not this provision of nature, by which things originally indifferent, but conducive to, or otherwise associated with, the satisfaction of our primitive desires, become in themselves sources of pleasure more valuable than the primitive pleasures' (*CW*, vol. X, p. 236). 'Conducive to or associated with' – in other words, things can only become parts of our happiness if they are in some way grounded in our natural desires and pleasures. And finally, Utilitarianism only recognizes as desirable those pleasures which do not excessively diminish other pleasures or cause an excess of pain, either to the individual or to others. This would rule out the pleasure the sadist gets in torturing his victims, and perhaps the pleasure the miser gets by hoarding his money instead of spending it on other enjoyments.

Is the Argument of *On Liberty* Logical?

The essay *On Liberty* also poses problems of interpretation, and has provoked a torrent of scholarly dispute (see especially Berger, 1984; Donner, 1991; Gray & Smith, 1991). I take the now orthodox view that the only way through the difficulties is to read the essay in the light of Mill's Utilitarianism, which is not contradicted by his defence of liberty as an end because, in the first place, liberty is not other than happiness: it is a part of happiness, naturally or chemically associated with pleasure. The human animal takes pleasure in untrammelled action, the free exercise of its faculties and the sense of power. Liberty is also valuable because it is intrinsically bound up with higher, active pleasures, including those of creation and self-creation. This is the subject of a whole chapter, 'Of individuality, as one of the elements of well-being'. The reader is advised that there is no substitute for reading the text itself, which is memorably eloquent: Mill was self-consciously a rhetorician as well as a logician, and he sets out to persuade the reader by conveying a vivid sense of the pleasure and dignity of free self-development, in accordance with one's natural bent and in defiance of mediocre conformity. He goes so far as to reach forward to Nietzsche in advocating 'Pagan self-assertion' as well as 'Christian self-denial'.

Such a similarity ought not to surprise us, for Mill, like Nietzsche, draws upon a romantic philosophy of the self elaborated in early nineteenth-century German thought. He acknowledges his debt to Wilhelm von Humboldt and, in the *Autobiography*, to Goethe; he learnt about this strand of German thinking also from Coleridge and Carlyle. He purveys to a British readership the idea and ideal of *Bildung*, of the unfolding and expression of the self's mix of powers and inclinations, through free and many-sided experience, and their combination into a rich, unique and coherent whole. This philosophy helps Mill to mount a challenge to the doctrine, long dominant in Western thought, that there is a single pattern of human excellence to which all should aspire. For Mill and the German theorists of *Bildung*, excellence can allow for variety.

Mention should also be made of another source of his ideal of liberty, at once classical and English. In his friend Grote's *History of Greece* Mill found an account of the Athenians under Pericles, 'the greatest people who have yet appeared on this planet', whose tolerance of individual diversity 'is most closely connected with the wonderful display of individual genius which made Athens illustrious, and with the comparative mediocrity of modern times' (*CW*, vol. XXV, pp. 1123, 1129; vol. XI, pp. 319–20). Mill admires the 'liberality and tolerance of Athenian social life', which underlines the point that the interference with liberty that most concerned him, especially in England, was that of public opinion rather than law. Mill goes so far as to praise eccentricity, an aspect of the essay which some Victorian critics thought went too far (*CW*, vol. XVIII, p. 269). But Mill connects eccentricity, and self-formation rather than slavish conformity, with a trait which Victorians greatly admired, namely strength of character (Collini, 1991, p. 93). Liberty then is not inconsistent with utility because it produces a host of good consequences, happiness in many forms.

It follows from this in the second place that liberty should often be protected, even when it immediately produces harm, because of the long-term good it promotes. What appears to be contrary to utility at first sight is consonant with it in the longer view. Wiser persons might interfere with people for their own good, to rescue them from self-damaging excesses: but in the long term they will be happier by learning from their own mistakes, attaining independence and strength of character; they will be happier knowing they are self-made, not manufactured by others. Consideration of the long-term in this way justifies free speech and 'experiments of living' (*CW*, vol. XVIII, p. 261). Free speech permits the propagation of error, and experiments in living may prove harmful to the experimenter: but an environment of free speech and experimentation is essential to discovery and progress, which in turn are likely to contribute to the diminution of misery and the growth of happiness. If error is proscribed, there is always the danger that elements of the truth will be banned too; for no authority can be sure of infallibility. In the third place, actions which detract from happiness should not always be prevented, because they are not always wrong. They are not wrong if they fall into the domains of prudence and aesthetics rather than morality. And they only come into the latter domain if it would be expedient to discourage them by means of sanctions, which once more invokes consideration of longer-term consequences.

So Mill's passion for liberty is not at odds with his Utilitarianism. But can a distinction between self- and other-regarding actions be elaborated, so as to provide a satisfactory defence of liberty as the 'simple principle' promised? The answer is that it can: but the elaboration reveals that the principle is not so simple. First and most important, when Mill writes about actions that affect or concern others, what he mostly (but not always) means is *actions which affect the interests of others* (some of his formulations actually say this – *CW*, vol. XVIII, p. 292) (Rees, 1960, pp. 113–29). Getting drunk, gambling or being idle may affect others in various ways but should not necessarily be prevented; in themselves they do not always harm the interests of others. But a man who regularly becomes violent when drunk may be placed under an injunction not to drink; and one whose idleness brings his children to want may be forced to work. In both of these cases the interests of others are affected by acts which otherwise would be self-regarding

(*CW*, vol. XVIII, p. 295). Protestants should not be prevented from eating pork in Muslim countries, nor Mormons from taking several wives. Mill finds the latter practice deplorable, but it is wrong to interfere with consenting adults for their own good (*CW*, vol. XVIII, p. 290). Great *offence* may be caused by pork-eating or polygamy, but *interests* have not been affected. I do not think that Mill is saying that Muslims and non-Mormons have not been rendered unhappy, or that their unhappiness does not count, or that 'morality-dependent harm', harm to a person because his peculiar moral convictions have been outraged, is to be ignored. Rather, a utilitarian calculation is going on here, and Mill thinks that in general the unhappiness of being offended is outweighed by other benefits (Honderich, 1982, pp. 506–7). By contrast, other benefits are in general unlikely to compensate for the affecting of people's interests. *In general* needs to be emphasized, for Mill allows exceptions. Public indecency, which offends others but does not harm their interests, may be forbidden. Presumably this is because the unhappiness of being prevented from taking one's clothes off in public weighs light in the scales of utilitarian calculation.

Refining *harm* as *harming interests* helps to get Mill's principle on the road, but raises a new problem: what does he mean by 'interests'? What is to be included in the list of 'interests' has been debated, and has consequences for the general interpretation of Mill's ideological stance. For example, Gray gives the vital interests as security and autonomy (Gray & Smith, 1991, p. 190) which supports a view of Mill as a classic non-interventionist liberal. Donner's list includes interests in self-development for all and sociability, yielding a more 'social-democratic', egalitarian Mill (Donner, 1991, pp. 181–3, 192).

In attempting to fill out Mill's list of interests, the last chapter of *Utilitarianism* helps without providing an exhaustive answer. The individual has an interest, for example, in security. This involves protection from harm to person and property. So an act which affected the person or property of another would not be a self-regarding act, and therefore it would be an open question whether state or society might intervene to prevent it. Intervention, however, would not be automatic. Whether or not to interfere with acts which harm the interests of others has to be decided with reference to utility. Trade is an important case in point. My economic activities may gravely affect the interests of others ('Trade is a social act', Mill concedes – *CW*, vol. XVIII, p. 293) if, for example, I cause them to become unemployed, or drive them out of business. But free trade, Mill thinks, is justified on other grounds, because it produces efficiency and prosperity; therefore interference with this class of other-regarding actions is not usually warranted.

Second, Mill will usually permit interference only with actions which *directly* harm others (*CW*, vol. XVII, p. 1832). Undoubtedly the reasoning behind this is utilitarian: indirectly an action might cause harm, but the benefit of preventing it is outweighed by the general benefits of liberty. Mill rightly thinks that it would be highly dangerous to liberty to prevent actions on the grounds that they *might* harm the interests of others; the potential scope for interference would be endless. Clear and present danger can alone justify infringements of liberty. So, for example, it would be wrong to prevent the sale of poisons because they might possibly be used to commit a murder (*CW*, vol. XVIII, pp. 293–4). It would be wrong to prevent the publication of a book or article arguing that corn-dealers are starvers of the poor, or that property is theft, on the grounds that the publication might inspire attacks on property: but if a man proclaimed such opinions to an excited mob in front of a corn-dealer's house, it would be right to arrest him. In the latter case, the expression of his opinions would be a positive instigation to a mischievous act (*CW*, vol. XVIII, p. 260).

Finally, interference is permitted not only to prevent positively harmful acts. The state, or society, may rightly interfere if an individual harms others by *failing* to act. It is right to punish a man who fails to bear his share of the common burdens (*CW*, vol. XVIII, p. 276).

Is *On Liberty* Extreme, or Covertly Illiberal?

Does Mill's defence of liberty go too far in the direction of individualism? Does it encourage people to think too much of themselves and too little of others? By leaving each to find their own good in their own way, does it fail to enforce standards? Is it a purely negative or neutral political philosophy which embodies no positive values? Would it in effect leave each individual to sink or swim, to flourish or go to perdition? Would it, by preventing the imposition of moral standards in private life by public opinion, lead to the corruption and disintegration of society? Conservative critics, best represented by the lawyers Fitzjames Stephen from the nineteenth century and Lord Devlin from the twentieth, have levelled such charges (Stephen, 1967; Devlin, 1965). Among many good arguments, one may be highlighted, namely Devlin's insistence that a recognized morality is just as important to a nation's

survival as a recognized government, and that public morality cannot
ignore what happens in private life. What, he asks, if half the population got drunk every night, or gambled, or became gay, or thought
adultery perfectly acceptable? Could society survive? What if Britain
had been a nation of debauchees in 1940? (Devlin, 1965, pp. 9–13, 17,
22, 111).

Without doubt there is a gulf between Devlin and Mill, opened up by a
profound difference over the scope of morality. Mill as we have seen
thinks that conduct falls within the domain of morality only if it is right to
encourage or discourage it by means of sanctions: and such sanctioning
is usually appropriate only if the conduct affects the interests of non-
consenting others. Therefore Mill's theoretical position was more radical
than that of the Wolfenden Report of 1957, which recommended the
legalisation of homosexuality and prostitution, and from which Lord
Devlin dissented. For Wolfenden recommended that certain immoral, but
private, acts should be tolerated by law. Mill's theory implies that drunk-
enness, gambling, homosexuality, adultery and prostitution are not in
themselves moral issues (Ryan, 1991, pp. 162–6). This is what his *theory*
implies: in practice his *judgements* are not always consistent with it, and it
is faintly anachronistic and out-of-character to suppose him gladly accept-
ing 'licentious' behaviour. When discussing the Contagious Diseases Acts
he referred to the use of prostitutes as 'illicit indulgence', 'vicious indulgence', 'questions of simple morality' (*CW*, vol. XXI, pp. 355–6, 360).

Generally speaking though, Mill's position is radical: Hampsher-
Monk judges it extraordinary (Hampsher-Monk, 1992, p. 369) and
Hart, Devlin's liberal opponent, thought Mill 'fantastic'. There has
been a rise of paternalism since Mill's day, which to an extent Hart
endorses on the grounds that we are less inclined to think that individuals know their own best interests, and that their choices are generally
free (Hart, 1963, p. 32). Mill would legalize the possession and also the
sale of all drugs, as in consistency he must: if I go to hell on heroin,
I affect nobody's interests but my own, unless I thereby incapacitate
myself for the performance of special duties. He would usually forbid
censorship, unless a spoken or printed utterance could clearly be
demonstrated to be a direct cause of harm to concrete interests. Not
only would he condemn Muslim attempts to silence Salman Rushdie:
I do not believe that Mill would have favoured the prosecution of those
who deny the holocaust or who publish racist arguments. But I am not
sure he would reject Andrea Dworkin's and Catherine MacKinnon's
recent proposals for legislation against pornography. It cannot be

proved that pornography causes sexual violence against women (or men for that matter), but pornographic images do not express opinions nor address the rational faculty. Mill's case is for freedom of thought and discussion, not for freedom to excite antisocial desires.

But essentially Mill's liberalism is not open to the charges levelled by Stephen and Devlin. A Millite Britain in 1940 would have been filled with self-disciplined patriots, modern heroes out of Plutarch, ready to fight and die. There is something curious here. Mill combines a classic, passionate defence of liberty with 'communitarian' themes of devotion to the common good and a concern to promote shared standards of morality.

Mill is a perfect Victorian in his commitment to altruism and unselfishness; nowhere is this clearer than in *Utilitarianism*, which at times sounds so like a sermon on charity that it comes as no surprise to find Mill insisting that 'In the golden rule of Jesus of Nazareth, we read the complete spirit of the ethics of utility. To do as one would be done by, and to love one's neighbour as oneself, constitute the ideal perfection of utilitarian morality' (*CW*, vol. X, p. 218). Nor is Mill content simply to recommend this disposition and hope it will prevail. He wants it fostered by education and opinion 'until, by the improvement of education, the feeling of unity with our fellow creatures shall be (what it cannot be doubted that Christ intended it to be)...deeply rooted in our character' (*CW*, vol. X, p. 227). There is a natural basis for this in the social feelings of humanity, the desire to be in unity with our fellow creatures; and Mill agrees with Comte that these sociable feelings are weak in primitive societies but get stronger as civilization advances. As time goes on, actions which once were thought to be exceptionally disinterested and benevolent come to be accepted as normal or even obligatory (*CW*, vol. X, p. 338). Here history does not appear to have confirmed Mill's predictions. He did not foresee how nationalism in the twentieth century would narrow rather than enlarge social sympathies, nor could he know how new technologies, such as the motor car and television, would lock people in private spaces.

The essay *On Liberty* is not merely a negative argument for non-interference: it is based upon a positive conception of the good. Liberty is good, Mill believes, not because it allows people to do just as they like, turn off their minds, relax and float downstream. It is good because it is bracing and invigorating, because it fosters strong characters and sturdy individuality and promotes progress. It is by no means clear that Mill's enthusiasm for liberty would be undimmed if it turned out that it produced weak, apathetic and sensual conformists. (A classic argument against Mill, voiced as early as 1859, is that discipline, not liberty, strengthens the character – Pyle, 1994, p. 22; Stephen, J.F., 1967, p. 83.) Nor does Mill recommend leaving people alone, to vegetate or deteriorate: they should actively be encouraged to develop what is best in them. To be sure, this is to be done by conviction and persuasion, not compulsion; but Mill thinks that individuals should be more ready to point out one another's follies and backslidings to a lower level of being (*CW*, vol. XVIII, p. 278).

Many find traces of illiberalism in the essay. Mill argues for legislation against producing too many children in a state threatened with over-population. In the light of recent developments in China and India, this no longer appears unthinkable: but he also argues for laws forbidding marriage 'unless the parties can show that they have the means of supporting a family' (*CW*, vol. XVIII, p. 304). Anyone who has seen Ken Loach's film *Ladybird, ladybird* will be worried by this, and it raises an important theoretical issue; throughout the essay (though not in other writings such as the *Political Economy* and the *Chapters on Socialism*), Mill largely ignores the relationship between liberty and the distribution of wealth and opportunity. This criticism of Mill is well put by McCloskey:

> The impoverished, unemployed person who, because he cannot secure work, suffers from malnutrition and disease, who would, if he could, marry the woman he loves, have a family, be creatively active in his chosen career ... but who because of his poverty is unable to do any of these things, is a slave compared with the well-paid worker in the modern liberal welfare state (McCloskey, 1971, p. 129).

Mill's essay neglects the possibility that liberty may be enlarged by increasing state activity rather than reducing it, nor is there any sense of the way in which entrenched concentrations of wealth and privilege can limit the liberty of the unprivileged by controlling their thoughts and opinions. Mill is afraid of the 'tyranny of the majority' in democratic societies, but fails (in this essay, though not elsewhere – *CW*, vol. XII, p. 166) to confront the danger that powerful minorities might manipulate and control the mass. He is horrified by the narrow, stifling conformism promoted by newspapers, the so-called organs of public opinion; but he does not ask about the extent to which their proprietors mould opinion. The thinking of the masses 'is done for them by men much like themselves, addressing them or speaking in their name, on the spur of the moment, through the newspapers' (*CW*, vol. XVIII, p. 269). The wording here implicitly rejects the idea that newspapers represent interests distinct from those of the mass, and that they consciously set about the business of forming the minds of their readers.

There is also an intractable difficulty about the legitimate scope of the 'social sanction', the punishment meted out by the disapproval of public opinion and its consequences. As remarked earlier, Mill is as much concerned to defend liberty against these informal pressures as he is to limit the formal interference of the state. The difficulty arises like this: think of some actions with which, according to the liberty principle, we may not interfere – the taking of dangerous drugs, compulsive and ruinous gambling, behaviour which is grossly ignoble and degrading, such as loutishness, gluttony or personal uncleanliness. But if we do not intervene we open ourselves to the charge of being uncaring, indifferent to others and their fate. Mill does not want this. He wants us to encourage others to improve themselves, and to live fully human, happy lives – happy in the higher sense. But how do you draw the line between helping and encouraging (good), and interfering (bad)? When does friendly advice turn into liberty-threatening pressure of public opinion?

> We have a right ... to act upon our unfavourable opinion of anyone ... We are not bound ... to seek his society; we have a right to avoid it ... We have a right, and it may be our duty, to caution others against him ... We may give others a preference over him in optional good offices (*CW*, vol. XVIII, p. 278).

Isn't this imposing a moral sanction against self-regarding acts, in contradiction of the liberty principle?

Therefore some have argued that there are elements of paternalism in Mill, or even that he was not a liberal at all. Generally speaking, such interpretations are strained, or based upon a narrow interpretation of liberalism. If a man who is committed to improving his fellow citizens is a paternalist, then Mill was one (Kurer, 1991, p. 6): but he explicitly repudiates *forcing* improvement upon adults. If a man who holds that they only are truly happy who are rationally self-directed towards 'higher' pleasures is not a liberal, then Mill was not one. But he forbade interference with the self-regarding conduct of those governed by appetite, or who pursue 'lower' pleasures. If it is illiberal to advocate self-control and the subordination of the impulses to the will, if this abolishes the distinction between liberty and discipline and turns the individual into a 'perfectly self-regulated panopticon' (Carlisle, 1991, pp. 205, 207), then Mill was illiberal: but the idea that liberty and self-control go hand-in-hand has been an enduring theme in Western thought. To say that Mill's willingness physically to prevent a man from crossing an unsafe bridge if there were no time to warn him (*CW*, vol. XVIII, p. 294) is forcing men to be free, or repressing their actual wills in the interest of their 'real' wills (Bosanquet, 1923, p. 65) is an unconvincing attempt to enlist Mill for a particular, and potentially totalitarian, conception of 'positive' freedom. Nor is Mill's liberalism suspect because he insists that choosing to sell oneself into slavery should not be permitted. It might be a self-regarding act, freely chosen: but the point of the simple principle is to *protect* liberty, not to enable individuals to give it up for ever.

Moral Motivation and Proof

A whole chapter is devoted to 'The Ultimate Sanction of the Principle of Utility', that is to say, to the question of moral motivation. One would not find such a chapter in present-day academic writings on moral philosophy, which largely confine themselves to questions about the meaning and logic of moral discourse. But it was a central issue for Mill's contemporaries, and for some time afterwards (Ryan, 1974, p. 96). They were especially concerned by his widely suspected repudiation of Christianity, and his advocacy of a 'religion of humanity' instead. How, they asked, could sinful humans be made moral if they no longer believed in hellfire? How could the selfish individuals of classic Utilitarianism ever be brought to serve a greater whole? (Stephen, J.F., 1967; Bradley, 1927, pp. 115–16; Willey, 1964, p. 185.) These questions troubled Mill, and he clearly felt the need to answer them. Moral motivation was also important to Mill because of his practical concerns – he wanted to improve the world. And finally his positivistic frame of mind placed the issue on the agenda. He wished to treat morality scientifically, to analyse and explain the facts of moral language and behaviour.

Mill thinks that those who care for others have endless sources of happiness, and that a principal cause of unhappiness is 'caring for nobody but themselves' (*CW*, vol. X, p. 215). There is a natural basis for altruism and morality: 'The idea of the pain of another is naturally painful; the idea of the pleasure of another is naturally pleasurable' (*CW*, vol. X, p. 60). Fellow-feeling is a natural human capacity (*CW*, vol. XV, p. 650). But in themselves these factors are not sufficient: 'the interest of each is indeed best promoted by the good of the whole, but no selfish person will ever know or believe this' (*CW*, vol. XV, p. 569). Mill therefore turns to the Benthamite theory of sanctions, but adds his own emphasis upon the internal sanction, the inner policeman, the conscience. He rightly thinks that external sanctions – the threat of punishment, the disapproval of our neighbours – would be of limited efficacity without the support of this inner one. Conscience is not natural, but acquired; it is a highly complex social and psychological phenomenon, a chemical union or association (*CW*, vol. XV, p. 649). In its finest form it is the result of a 'moral culture' mediated through eloquence rather than logic. In two separate discussions of Plato's *Gorgias*, Mill insists that men and women cannot be persuaded to love virtue by rational argument; it is 'caught by inspiration or sympathy', 'breathe[d] into us through our imagination and our sensations' (*CW*, vol. XI, pp. 149–50, 416).

Mill's determination to be scientific and empirical about morality determines the manner of the 'proof' of the principle of Utility in the next chapter. It is significant that the 'proof' follows the exploration of moral feelings; Mill wants to get the facts of moral phenomena straight first. Given that moral principles cannot strictly be proved, his strategy is to remind the reader of known facts about people's desires which will persuade them that happiness is the ultimate good and which will bring them to agree with him about the essential constituents of happiness. This is a continuation of Mill's argument against intuitionism, which we saw was a central intention of his *Logic* and later *Examination of Sir William Hamilton's Philosophy*. According to intuitionism, we directly intuit that certain things are good, or that certain actions are right and others wrong. Like Bentham, Mill thought that alleged moral intuitions were not objective knowledge: rather they were expressions of personal preference or prejudice, having a conservative tendency.

So Mill appeals to evidence instead: but it is not easy to be convinced that the evidence proves him right. His moral theory is based upon a substantive account of human nature. He does not say that all humans are born longing for higher pleasures, including the pleasures of independence; he knows that these desires are acquired. But he believes that all human beings, if given the opportunity, *will* acquire these desires and, in an atmosphere of free thought and discussion, will concur in preferring them. But is liberty, for example, an essential part of the happiness of all humans? Or is it vital only from the viewpoint of Western liberal individualism? A different viewpoint might produce a different conception of the good. An American Indian might consider that his primary good lay in the preservation of his nomadic and tribal way of life in harmony with nature, a way of life which Western liberal individualism destroys. Or an Islamic fundamentalist might think that his deepest desire was to live in an Islamic state under Islamic law, and that Western freedom is decadent and immoral. Mill of course would detest this as religious tyranny. But what right has he to privilege *his* conception of the good over that of the American Indian or Islamic fundamentalist? It is not enough to answer that conceptions of the good other than Mill's will, 'when intellectual culture goes on, yield by degrees to the dissolving force of analysis' (*CW*, vol. X, pp. 213, 230–1). This sounds like arguing that those who acquire Western liberal mental habits embrace Western liberal values.

Even within the framework of Western liberalism, Mill's Utilitarianism is contestable. Utilitarianism is the moral philosophy of the impartial observer or disinterested law-giver who, standing outside and above society, judges what will be best for the whole. A major rival to this is the 'social contract' discourse, of Hobbes, Locke and Rousseau and of Rawls in this century. This takes the point of view of the involved subject, who bargains with other subjects with a view, not to maximizing the general good but rather to securing a fair deal for herself. The social contract approach avoids the dangers of aggregate Utilitarianism. Aggregation, as already indicated, opens up the possibility of sacrificing the one or the few for the sake of the many: the social contract, which insists upon fairness to each and every individual, categorically rules that out.

The dangers of aggregation are also avoided by taking indefeasible rights, rights which cannot be defeated or set aside by an appeal to some other moral principle, as the starting point. If for example there is a right to life and it is the primary right, then no appeal to the greatest happiness can justify taking a life. We may kill only to protect life, in self-defence or the defence of others. This could be invoked against capital punishment, as a captured and imprisoned murderer is no longer a threat. It was entirely consistent with Mill's Utilitarianism that he spoke in parliament in favour of the death penalty. To execute a convicted murderer might be in accordance with utility, even if consideration were confined to the murderer himself: the brief terror and pain of death might be less than the long-drawn out misery of life imprisonment. When questions of deterrence are brought into the equation, the death penalty promises further benefits (*CW*, vol. XVI, p. 987). A Utilitarian insensitivity to rights is also exhibited in his youthful defence of 'resurrection-men' who steal bodies for dissection: if 'no one knows that the body of his friend or relative has been taken', then what harm is done? (*CW*, vol. XXII, p. 50).

Natural, indefeasible or ultimate rights were suspect to Mill just as intuitionism was suspect. The claim that each individual desires happiness is a factual assertion which can be tested by reference to experience: the claim that each individual has an indefeasible right to life does not appear to be a factual statement at all. It could simply be an expression of a widely held prejudice, and to Mill prejudices were reprehensible, conservative and anti-progressive. But it might be argued that tradition and prejudice are central to moral discourse and behaviour, and that in discarding them we risk losing everything. Clearly, we do not have rights in the same way as we have hands and feet, or desires for that matter. But we have rights by custom and tradition, and in this sense they are 'facts'. If they have been valued for generations and are valued now by millions, this may be sufficient to 'prove' them.

In conclusion it can be said that over a century of criticism has failed to demolish Mill's 'scientific' Utilitarianism and defence of liberty. A logical and sophisticated theory can be elicited from his writings, one which is plausible and appealing. On the other hand, Mill has failed in his ambition to drive other competitors from the field; for example, rights-based and contractual ethics remain serious contenders. There is also the possibility that Utilitarianism (and by the same token contractualism and rights) is time- and culture-bound, having no purchase outside modern Western civilization. Perhaps we are compelled to recognize a plurality of moral discourses, which cannot wholly be reconciled: a conclusion at which Mill would have been appalled.

5

POLITICS

Political Activism

In 1865 Mill was invited to stand for parliament for the Westminster constituency, which had a radical pedigree and which had been Liberal since 1832, with the sole exception of 1841 when one of its two seats had gone Conservative. Mill accepted, pleased at the prospect of a 'taller pulpit' for the propagation of his ideas (*CW*, vol. XVI, p. 1165). His terms were unusual and principled. He would not be a spokesman for local interests; he would not canvass; he would not bribe or treat and would not spend any of his own money on the campaign; and when in parliament he would propose votes for women. It was said at the time that God himself could not be elected on such a programme. Mill *was* elected, after a brief campaign of public meetings in one of which he admitted, before a working-class audience and to a burst of applause, that he had written that the working classes were generally liars. Both Mill and his Whig running mate Grosvenor received over 4,500 votes: the 'Liberal-Conservative' W.H. Smith, received 700 fewer. Mill's first three speeches to the house were failures; Disraeli wickedly remarked, 'Ah, I see, the finishing governess'. But his fourth speech, on the Liberal Reform Bill of 1866, was a triumph, and thereafter he was a prominent parliamentarian who raised the tone of debate (Stephen, L, 1912, p. 64).

After the passing of the Conservative Reform Act of 1867, there was a general election and Mill stood again for Westminster. The campaign was bitter and polarized: Mill was lampooned in the conservative press, but received at well-attended meetings with rapturous applause and much waving of hats and handkerchiefs (*CW*, vol. XXVIII, pp. 320, 341, 359). An election song dubbed him 'The people's soldier in woe and weal' and ended 'Hurrah for *Worth* and the *Brains* lads,/ And a triple hurrah for Mill' (Kent, 1978, p. 34). But the conservative W.H. Smith topped the poll by over 1,000, Grosvenor was returned and Mill lost. Because the liberals made considerable gains elsewhere under the newly extended franchise, it has been said that the stands he took in and out of parliament caused his defeat. Mill blamed, among other things, the better organization and deeper purse of his opponent. He remarked that two groups with whom he was associated, the candidates of the working class and the intellectuals, the university liberals who had done well in 1865, were defeated everywhere (*CW*, vol. XVI, pp. 1486, 1488, 1495–6). Grosvenor, who got nine more votes than Mill in 1865, only got 300 more in 1867; perhaps we should conclude that Mill's principles lost him rather less than 300 votes. In the election of 1874 the conservatives handsomely won both seats, establishing a new pattern in Westminster. Clearly, the complexion of the seat had changed, and no doubt if two conservatives had stood in 1867 instead of one, Grosvenor would have been ousted too. After his defeat Mill was offered more than one safe seat, but he declined; he was happy to retire to Avignon, to his botanizing and writing. The first fruit was his essay on *The Subjection of Women* in 1869. He continued to be active in campaigns for women's suffrage and for land tenure reform, remarking that 'the emancipation of women, and co-operative production, are...the two great changes that will regenerate society' (*CW*, vol. XVII, p. 1535).

This decade of Mill's life, embracing his period in parliament and his principal political writings, raises several important questions. Exactly where did Mill stand? Was he radical, even socialist, or somewhat conservative? Was he, in theory and in practice, a democrat? Does he deserve his place in the feminist pantheon? Was he a successful politician, or an ineffectual, ivory-tower philosopher? These questions require to be discussed in a manner which avoids anachronism, by the standards of his time, not by late twentieth-century conceptions. Four aspects of his thought and practice especially merit consideration: empire, democracy, socialism and women. If we are to understand him properly, we need first to explore some of the fundamental ideas and attitudes which shaped his thinking on these issues.

Fundamental Ideas

According to present-day conceptions, Mill was an out-and-out 'modernist' in political mentality. He situated himself in a grand historical narrative of progress and was convinced that the future belonged to those who thought as he did. In part it is a standard 'Enlightenment' narrative of the progressive triumph of reason, science and impartial truth over the dark forces of ignorance, prejudice and corrupt interests. Mill also employs the standard Enlightenment categorization of ascending levels: savagery, barbarism and civilization. He constructs the past as brutal, animal, violent; the emerging future is orderly and rational. Civilization advances by conquering nearly all of the natural instincts (*CW*, vol. XIV, pp. 26–7). In the pre-Christian era, the triumph of the Greeks over the Persians and the ascendancy of Athens over Sparta was the victory of civilization over barbarism, of intellect over brute force (*CW* , vol. XI, p. 321) and, if Athens had not finally been defeated, perhaps liberty would be a thousand years further forward. This dualism not only distinguished one nation from another: it also distinguished between two parts of the self, the lower animal part and the higher human part. We might wonder whether Mill was right to divide the human self in this way, and to place so low a value on its 'animal' component. It impairs his attitude to sex and to the population question: as Bain put it, 'in the so-called sensual feelings, he was below average … he made light of the difficulty of controlling the sexual appetite' (Bain, 1882, p. 149).

This animal/human dualism informs his perception of his own society. Into it was woven what one is tempted to call a middle-class contrast between aristocracy and meritocracy (*CW*, vol. XXI, pp. 272–3), were it not for the fact that Mill's letters and journalism suggest that he never identified himself as middle class, much less with commerce but rather, more traditionally, as a gentleman. He detested the landed aristocracy and squirearchy, the boneheads who support the 'stupidest party', as he infamously dubbed the Conservatives (*CW*, vol. XXVIII, pp. 85–6). The ascendancy of aristocracy was based upon the rule of force; that of meritocracy results from the steady growth of the rule of law. The Spartans were an aristocracy, the Athenians democratic.

Not that aristocrats were his only target. Mill and Harriet waged a press campaign against brutality in the 1840s and 1850s, which he continued in the House of Commons. They were pioneers in putting the violence of husbands against wives on the political agenda, but also highlighted that of parents (including women) against children, of men against animals, and of employers (again including women) against servants. They often but not always equated *brutal* with *poor*. For example, they argued that imprisonment, even with solitary confinement or hard labour, would be little worse than the ordinary lot of the ruffianly part of the population who beat their wives. Therefore they recommended corporal punishment and wrote of the need to 'unbrutalize' the people (*CW*, vol. XXI, pp. 105–8): 'In this I acted chiefly as amanuensis to my wife' (*CW*, vol. XXI, p. 102). Mill's articles on Ireland in the 1840s depict the starving peasants as little better than savages, incapable of controlling their sexual appetites, and he once wrote of Welsh peasants as 'sensual & stupid boor[s]' (*CW*, vol. XIII, p. 452). But the letters convey the impression that in his later years Mill's regard for working men grew (*CW*, vol. XVI, pp. 1103, 1205–6; vol. XVII, pp. 1759, 1870).

Mill's conviction that reason, humanity and history were on his side aligns him with late nineteenth-century Fabianism, and indeed with the British left in general before it lost confidence in the late 1970s. This overweening smugness still arouses the hatred of conservatives such as Maurice Cowling. The very business of pointing out these foundations of Mill's political thought immediately casts doubt on any assessment of him as a conservative, arousing the suspicion that any such categorization must be anachronistic. As Mill explained in his election speeches of 1865 and in his *Autobiography*, he was a midwife of history, a scout or advance guard, one who sat by the cradle of all the great political reforms (*CW*, vol. XXVIII, p. 15):

> I have never been one of those who have left things alone when they have been an uphill fight, but I have left them when the fight was no longer difficult. ... I have left that prosperous thing, and have turned to something else – to something that was still a crotchet, still an abstraction, still something that no practical person would battle with (*CW*, vol. XXVIII, p. 16).

He presented himself to his electors as 'the candidate of advanced liberalism' (*CW*, vol. XXVIII, p. 22). He thought it his mission to take up the causes which were too radical and unpopular for 'advanced liberals' such as Gladstone to risk. The radical should not simply wait for public opinion and the average man (*CW*, vol. XIV, p. 68): there were times when it was right to speak out, for example on the state of Ireland in 1868. In relation to Hare's plan for proportional representation, he was inspired 'to fight the uphill battle of unpopular opinions, in a public arena, against superior numbers' (*CW*, vol. XXVIII, pp. 254, 183).

This makes Mill sound eccentric, fringe, impractical; but he did not always parade his own superior rectitude regardless of the offence caused to less enlightened hearers. His radicalism was held in tension with a Burkean sense of politics as the art of the possible, flowing from the historical lessons learnt from the 'Germano-Coleridgean school'. Though a fully paid-up member of the party of progress, he was self-consciously not utopian. Not all of the good is possible immediately; the radical needs to know what is the next stage in order, and work for that (*CW*, vol. XII, p. 48). He told his constituents that 'I would not object to accept any reasonable compromise which would give me even a little of that of which I hope in time to obtain the whole' (*CW*, vol. XXVIII, p. 23). As a political actor Mill had an acute sense of the need to be at once courageous and a wise tactician (*CW*, vol. VI, p. 354). He praised the nineteenth-century French liberal Guizot as 'a model of the consistency of a statesman as distinguished from … a fanatic', who prudently 'lets some of his maxims go to sleep while the time is unpropitious for asserting them' (*CW*, vol. XIII, pp. 454–5). We can only see a certain distance ahead, therefore we must be tentative, and promote the beneficial changes which are already in partial progress, already in the minds of the more intelligent and active (*CW*, vol. XVII, p. 1873). Accordingly, he was perfectly prepared to be reticent about convictions whose expression could do his causes no good, such as those on contraception, divorce and religion. Convinced as he was that the progressive forces had found their leader in Gladstone, Mill took care not to embarrass the precarious Liberal government of 1865–6 by the expression of unpopular opinions. Mill sought, like all principled politicians who wish to achieve anything, to cut a course between idealism and pragmatism (Kinzer, Robson & Robson, 1992).

Mill's reputation is as a thinker; but we shall never fully understand his thought if we fail to recognize that he was always politically engaged and had a strong sense of himself as a shrewd strategist. Mill speaks as a logician but also, steeped as he was in the classics and in Aristotle from early childhood, as a rhetorician, one interested not only in the truth but also in persuasion for political ends. Bain wrote of his 'power of persuasion' and 'tact in discerning what would suit the persons addressed' (Bain, 1882, p. 184). It is vital to take Margaret Canovan's advice seriously when reading him, looking carefully for the shifts between logic and rhetoric, between those passages where Mill speaks his whole mind, and those where he addresses a historically specific audience with a view to their conversion (Canovan, 1987, p. 520).

Imperialism

Mill was no pacifist (*CW*, vol. XIII, pp. 728–9), but he thought national selfishness as unacceptable as individual (*CW*, vol. XXI, p. 114). He hoped for a United States of Europe, but judged it would be long in coming (*CW*, vol. XVII, p. 1800). He was not opposed to a British Empire, believing it important for Britain's prestige and the liberty she stood for (*CW*, vol. XV, p. 784; vol. XVI, pp. 1108–9). With the diplomat Edward Gibbon Wakefield (1796–1862), to whose ideas he was indebted, he thought that the white settler colonies were an invaluable outlet for surplus population and capital (Sullivan, 1983, pp. 607–9). He inherited from his Benthamite mentors the anti-paternalist maxim that individuals are the best judges of their own interests and that therefore they should enjoy liberty and self-government. But this maxim was meant to apply 'only to human beings in the maturity of their faculties' (*CW*, vol. XVIII, p. 224); to adults, not children, to civilized human beings, not barbarians. Consequently, Mill was not opposed to an advanced country paternally ruling a backward one (*CW*, vol. XXI, pp. 118–19). In all consistency, imperial administrator as he was, he could not think otherwise. But he was no racist; he did not think there were natural racial characteristics, nor that certain peoples were inherently and eternally backward (*CW*, vol. XV, p. 899). The imperial relationship was for him primarily a moral one; it was legitimate to rule another people, only if that rule was exercised for their good. Therefore he thought that an imperial power should take steps to improve its subjects, and as they improved they should participate in their own government; eventually they would become largely self-governing, perhaps as dependencies, as had happened to Canada.

In spite of the fact that his working life was spent at East India House, the *Autobiography* makes very little reference to India. His precise opinions on that subject, and how they evolved, are not easy to establish, for the despatches he wrote on the relationship between the company and the princes, which was his area of responsibility, were collective efforts produced in an interchange of views. But careful reading, aided by letters and other texts, gives some idea of his stance. Zastoupil argues that after Mill's father's death in 1836, the younger Mill adopted a different approach to that of the older. James Mill was a firm westernizing reformer who thought that the company should act as an enlightened despot in India; he paid little regard to Indian cultural traditions and patriotic feelings. He thought that Indians, if well governed, did not care whether their rulers wore turbans or hats. John Stuart Mill also thought that ordinary Indians preferred being ruled by the British (*CW*, vol. XV, p. 561). Influenced however not only by German and French historical thinking but also by a group of Indian administrators inspired by Burkean Whiggism, he recognized that reforming ambitions had to be tempered by a sensitivity to the feelings and opinions of the native population (Zastoupil, 1994: for an alternative view see Moore, 1983; Majeed, 1996). He was appalled by Macaulay's imposition of the English language in Indian education (*CW*, vol. XVII, p. 1970). But his cultural tolerance never went as far as an acceptance of the equal validity of Hindu culture. It might be necessary to proceed cautiously and respectfully, but the goal remained the modernization and enlightenment of India.

He sincerely believed that the East India Company governed in the interests of the Indians, and was 'the *protector* of the natives of India against the avarice & domineering spirit of rapacious European adventurers' (*CW*, vol. XVII, p. 1983). He was horrified by the atrocities perpetrated by the English in revenge for the Indian Mutiny (*CW*, vol. XVI, p. 1205), and he thought that the move to abolish the East India Company stemmed from a perception that it defended the natives and refused to favour white residents (*CW*, vol. XXX, pp. 81–2). In his last years he sensed that a new and disgraceful imperial spirit was in the ascendant – insolent, bullying, contemptuous of 'inferior races' (*CW*, vol. XVII, pp. 1560, 1599, 1686).

Ireland

Mill never favoured self-government, let alone independent statehood, for Ireland (*CW*, vol. VI, pp. 507–32). He thought that from England's point of view it would be dangerous to have so close an independent and perhaps hostile neighbour, a potential ally and bridgehead for a foreign enemy. For the Irish, continued membership of a larger, wealthier and powerful nation offered manifold benefits. But Mill knew that British rule in Ireland had always failed and was still failing when measured against his ideal of empire. Two crises focused his attention on Ireland: the potato famine of the mid-1840s, in the aftermath of which millions died or emigrated, and the Fenian violence of the mid-1860s.

Mill's series of forty-three *Morning Chronicle* articles on the condition of Ireland in 1846 and 1847 makes fascinating and uncomfortable reading. He had long thought of Ireland as a Malthusian nightmare (*CW*, vol. XXVI, p. 305). He depicted the Irish peasants as semi-animal, idle and fecund, ever ready to 'people up', as he put it, to the food supply. Their degradation was not a racial characteristic, but a consequence of land tenure patterns; they were insecure, rackrented leaseholders while the prudent and virtuous continental peasants Mill admired so much were independent landholders. He was utterly opposed to solving the problem by outdoor relief, even for the emergency: that would 'bid fair to imbue the whole labouring population with the feelings of sturdy beggars' (*CW*, vol. XXVI, p. 972). He retailed the story that when Lord John Russell's government gave outdoor relief in return for public works such as roadmaking, whole districts gave up cultivation; the Irish poor would rather subsist on government handouts in return for a little light stonebreaking than engage in the heavy labour of digging and planting their own fields: 'The whole Irish people are rushing with one impulse to fasten themselves upon the taxes' (*CW*, vol. XXVI, p. 978). Mill was committed to relief only within the workhouse according to the principle of less eligibility: and since the condition of employed labourers in Ireland was very poor, that implied a very low standard of relief.

If Mill's present-day admirers are depressed by this, they can take comfort from his long-term solution. He proposed that the uncultivated wastes should be drained and divided into small farms of ten acres in order to create a class of independent peasants, either proprietors or with fixity of tenure at fair rents. He was bitterly opposed to state-subsidized schemes of waste cultivation which would simply give more land to the landlords – for it was the landlords who had failed, and caused Ireland's plight. He did not favour the English pattern for Ireland, of large and profitable farms created by clearing the tenants off the land: 'it is the one and not the hundred who ought to depart' (*CW*, vol. XXVI, p. 896). Mill's solution was not adopted: the landlords got the land, with the help of public money (*CW*, vol. XXVIII, pp. 252–3). There can be little doubt that this experience pushed Mill towards his final position, of opposition to the absolute right of private property, and in favour of measures of land nationalization.

In 1865 the Fenians, founded in America and dedicated to an Irish republic, became active in Britain. In 1866 the government brought in a bill to suspend *habeas corpus* in Ireland. Mill drew considerable hostility upon himself by speaking on the occasion and 'denouncing...the English mode of governing Ireland...any attack on what Fenians attacked was looked upon as an apology for them' (*CW*, vol. I, p. 277). In 1867 he spoke in a deputation to Lord Derby, the Conservative Prime Minister, to secure the commutation of the death sentence on a convicted Fenian (*CW*, vol. XVIII, pp. 165–7).

Mill's pamphlet 'England and Ireland' of 1868, and his major House of Commons speech on that subject in the same year, set out his analysis of Irish discontent and the proposed remedy, developing the themes of his 1840s articles. The pamphlet is more radical than the speech, an example of Mill's political realism and conciliatory tactics as an orator. Land tenure was the root of the problem: absentee and exploitative landlords, rackrenting, insecurity of tenure and failure to compensate tenants for the improvements they made. The answer was to create a secure and prosperous peasantry by permanent tenure at fair fixed rents, paid to the landlords if they were prepared to accept the terms, or otherwise to the state which would buy the landlords out. Without this, Mill predicted, Ireland would rebel and become an independent republic: and the Irish would be right. The East India Company, at the instigation of Mill's father, had pursued such a policy in India; but Indian landlords could more easily be ignored than Anglo-Irish ones. Mill was compared to Jack Cade and denounced as 'the most recent and most thoroughgoing apostle of Communism' (Kinzer, Robson & Robson, 1992, pp. 174–7): and indeed he had written that 'revolutionary measures are the thing now required' (*CW*, vol. VI, p. 518).

Jamaica

Mill's unpopularity over Ireland pales beside the wrath he drew upon himself over Jamaica. There, 13,000 whites ruled 420,000 exploited and impoverished blacks. There was a localized black uprising in October 1865, which killed a score of whites. Eyre, the Governor, declared martial law in the affected part, executed 439 after trials which often were travesties of justice, flogged many more including women, and burned a thousand homes. A Jamaica Committee was formed in England, with the object of securing the condemnation of Eyre (who had been relieved of his post) and compensation for his victims. Mill, who became chair of the committee in July 1866, thought that Eyre and some of his associates should be tried for murder.

The cause became a passion for him: he could see what most of his countrymen denied or ignored, that British imperialism itself was on trial. His allies included prominent scientists and social scientists: Harrison, Beesly, Dicey, Green, Thorold Rogers, Darwin, Huxley, Lyle and Spencer. His enemies included great names in the field of literature – Kingsley, Ruskin, Tennyson, Dickens and Carlyle. The Eyre affair was a defining moment in British politics. It was a staging-post in the rise of a triumphalist and neo-Darwinist conception of empire quite different from Mill's moral imperialism. Conservative defenders of Eyre associated the rising of the Jamaican blacks with the Indian mutiny, the victory of the American North over Southern 'gentlemen', Fenian and Trade Union violence and the onward march of democracy (Semmel, 1962, p. 59). For them Mill was on all the wrong sides. The anti-Eyre cause was strongly supported by British protestant dissent, horrified at the judicial murder of black Baptists and Methodists. And it may have focused a tension between the 'domestic manliness' which Mill represented and the aggressive masculinity of late-Victorian imperialism (Hall, 1992, pp. 255–85).

In the end, no English magistrate or Grand Jury would commit white men to the courts for having killed a few hundred Afro-Carribeans. Many thought that Mill was vindictively persecuting a hero; some of his own committee thought that prosecuting Eyre would make him a martyr. The Anglican clergyman and novelist Charles Kingsley was of the opinion that the blacks deserved all they got for being heathen, and Carlyle, Victorian sage and author of 'The Nigger Question' (which Mill called 'a true work of the devil', *CW*, vol. XXI, p. 95) remarked 'Poor Eyre! ... Such his reward for saving the West Indies, and hanging one incendiary mulatto, well worth the gallows, if I can judge' (Packe, 1954, p. 469). Mill's stand brought him abusive letters and threats of assassination (*CW*, vol. XVI, p. 1405). The Gladstone government paid Eyre's legal expenses in 1872 (Mill exclaimed 'after this ... I shall wish for a Tory Government', *CW*, vol. XVII, p. 1829) and the subsequent Tory government restored Eyre's pension.

Democracy

In the *Autobiography* Mill informs us that in the late 1840s and 1850s he and Harriet were 'much less democrats than I had been' (*CW*, vol. I, p. 239), and that when he entered parliament in 1865 'as I had shown in my political writings that I was aware of the weak points in democratic opinions, some Conservatives…had not been without hopes of finding me an opponent of democracy'. But as we read on we find him insisting that his doubts about democracy did not add up to a rejection of it. An immediate move to pure democracy would not be desirable; some sections of the working classes were not ready for it and a system must be devised to safeguard against its problems, but he 'unhesitatingly decided in its favour' (*CW*, vol. I, p. 288).

If we turn to the articles written in 1835 and 1840 on 'Tocqueville on Democracy in America' at the height of Mill's alleged conservative period, we find the same. Mill is more pro-democracy than Tocqueville, and does not do full justice to the Frenchman's doubts (Hamburger, 1976, pp. 120–4). Mill thought that he differed from earlier radicals in doubting that democracy was the best system for all peoples at all times, and he had a rich sense of the downside of democracy. Nevertheless he presents himself and Tocqueville as *defenders* of democracy, which they both believed inevitable. He distinguishes democratic institutions from democratic society, and his worries are principally about the latter. Democratic society is characterized by equality of conditions, in itself a good thing but having a tendency to promote mediocrity and conformity. Even these evils are the result of modernity, of progress and mass society rather than of equality itself. And democratic institutions may offer a corrective to some of the evils of democratic society (*CW*, vol. XVIII, pp. 159, 191–2).

The French Revolution of 1848 inspired Mill with a high regard for the artisans of Paris: 'the most intelligent and best-conducted labouring class…to be found on the earth's surface' and it fanned his enthusiasm for democracy. The first volume of Grote's *History of Greece* had recently appeared, and from it Mill had taken an ideal of liberal, tolerant democracy in Periclean Athens (*CW*, vol. XX, pp. 334, 359; vol. XXV, pp. 1104–5, 1112, 1123). But the installation in France of the jingoistic dictatorship of Napoleon III on the basis of repeated democratic plebiscites deeply depressed him and caused him to doubt the wisdom of giving votes to illiterate peasants: 'None are so illiberal, none so bigoted in their hostility to improvement, none so superstitiously attached to the stupidest and worst of old forms and usages, as the uneducated' (*CW*, vol. XIX, p. 327). This is the determining context of his proposals for restraining and controlling democracy in *Representative Government* of 1861, and of *Thoughts on Parliamentary Reform* of 1859 which is the high-water mark of his doubts about universal suffrage. Especially in the 1850s then, Mill feared that democracy would come too quickly (*CW*, vol. XXVI, p. 662). But the American Civil War began in 1861; Mill became impassioned about it as a heroic crusade against slavery. It gave him new faith in American democracy and in those sections of the British working class who supported the North while their 'betters' supported the South, even though the North's blockade of Southern cotton had thrown them out of work (*CW*, vol. XXI, pp. 130, 142; vol. XV, p. 813). Mill always thought of himself as a democrat, in the sense that democratic institutions, carefully constructed, were his ultimate and not remote ideal.

This, however, does not provide a definitive answer to the question, 'was Mill a democrat?' For we might conclude that Mill was simply mistaken, and that the institutions he advocated were not democratic at all. This is a complex and contentious issue; the literature debating the nature and definition of democracy is now enormous. In order to simplify and set a framework for the discussion, four issues may be signalled. First, we might take the essence of democracy to be very simple: all that is required is that everybody has a vote, and that a genuine choice is offered, i.e., not as in some one-party states where there is only one candidate. Second, democracy might be specified as *political equality*: all have an equal say in determining how they are governed. Third, we must pay attention to the ideas of radical democrats who insist upon direct and frequent participation if a system is to be judged democratic. Fourth, sensitivity to history is required: Mill must not be assessed by 'timeless' standards, if there are any such, but must be thought of in relation to democracy as it was conceived in the nineteenth century.

Like his father and Bentham, Mill thought that a principal argument for democracy was in terms of self-protection: individuals tend to promote their own interests, and in a non-democratic system those who hold political power will advance their own interests at the expense of the powerless. This is the main ground on which Mill demands votes for women: there is no other way in which they can protect themselves against the tyranny of men. But he was vividly aware that people can only be counted upon to use the vote to defend their interests if they have a sound knowledge of them. Some may be too ignorant or shortsighted, and in their case the self-protection argument for enfranchisement is undermined. Therefore less advanced peoples, such as the majority of the population of the Indian subcontinent, were not ready for democracy. For the same reason, some individuals in advanced civilizations should not be enfranchised: Mill would exclude those who do not have a basic proficiency in reading, writing and arithmetic.

Mill's argument for this exclusion is by no means a bad one: if a person cannot read, then how, in a society where communication of politically relevant information is mainly by the printed word, can he or she know how to use a vote? (*CW*, vol. XVIII, p. 31). He did not wish the exclusion to be insuperable or permanent, thinking that the state should compel parents to have their children educated in basic literacy and numeracy, giving them financial assistance where necessary. But if the defining test of a democrat is supporting adult suffrage, then Mill fails that test. His argument for exclusion was better in the mid-nineteenth century than it is now: today television and radio have taken over from newspapers as the main media for communicating politically relevant information.

Mill goes further down this road, arguing that though all who have attained a basic level of education should have a voice, they should not have an equal voice 'until all are equal in worth as human beings' (*CW*, vol. XIX, p. 323). Votes should be weighed as well as counted, and therefore additional votes should be given to those with higher intellectual attainments, such as a degree or a professional qualification. This is meat and drink to those who contend that Mill was no democrat. It is true that he insisted there should be no property qualification for political power as in the pre-democratic British political system: but, as critics have pointed out, the higher educational qualifications would tend to correlate with wealth, especially in the nineteenth century. This recommendation contradicts the political equality which some have seen as the essence of democracy. In Mill's defence it should be remembered that 'fancy franchises' of this kind were 'in the air' in the 1850s and 1860s and were proposed in several abortive reform bills (Kent, 1978, p. 44). In his *Autobiography* he wrote that extra votes would only be feasible

> after the establishment of a systematic National Education by which the various grades of politically valuable acquirement may be accurately defined and authenticated. Without this it will always remain liable to strong, possibly conclusive, objections; and with this, it would perhaps not be needed (*CW*, vol. I, p. 262).

In 1870 he publicly declared that the poor should be given more education than the '3Rs': 'In education there is no such thing as

"too much" ' (*CW*, vol. XXIX, p. 399). His advocacy of educational qualifications rests upon the eminently defensible idea that in a democracy
political education designed to produce knowledgeable and effective
democrats is essential. On the other hand, he thought that it would be
bad if a lettered and cultivated class dominated unchecked. He was not
with Plato an advocate of 'philosopher kings': no rulers, no matter how
well educated, are infallible and the people are not so imbecile as to be
incapable of 'calling their scientific ruler to account' (*CW*, vol. XX,
p. 270; vol. XI, p. 436).

There is a less defensible exclusion. In accordance with the principle
laid down by his father of preventing power from falling into the hands
of a fraction of society whose interest is contrary to that of society as a
whole, Mill would give the vote only to those who pay taxes and are
sensible of paying them. Non-tax payers would be tempted to raise
public spending recklessly, spending other people's money upon themselves. Merely paying indirect taxes on tea, coffee, sugar, tobacco and
alcohol would not suffice to check profligacy. Mill proposes a poll tax in
order to make voters aware of the consequences of their spending
wishes. And anyone who is receiving public money in relief of poverty,
or who has received such relief during the past five years, should tem-
porarily be disfranchised (*CW*, vol. XIX, pp. 471–2). Mill had already
proposed these disqualifications in 1835, in a list which also included
those convicted of a criminal offence and anyone seen drunk during
the previous year (*CW*, vol. XVIII, pp. 31–2).

It is difficult to see how these exclusions could reasonably be
defended, even in the mid-nineteenth century. Those in receipt of poor
relief are still obliged to obey laws and may be called upon to fight for
their country, to which, Mill asserted earlier, they should be entitled to
give or withhold their consent through voting (*CW*, vol. XIX, p. 469).
And a person might be in receipt of public relief through no fault of his
or her own, because of involuntary unemployment or chronic illness. It
would not do to reply that such persons ought to save or insure against
such eventualities; not all wages were high enough to permit saving or
the payment of high premiums.

Mill had broader worries about class or sectional legislation in a
democracy. This marks him off from his father, who simplisti-
cally thought that votes for all (men) would imply rule in the interests
of all. The younger Mill recognized that even with universal suffrage a
majority of whites might oppress a minority of negroes, a majority of
Catholics might oppress a minority of Protestants (*CW*, vol. XIX,

p. 442). A majority of the poor, or of unskilled labourers, ignorant of the truths of political economy, might legislate against the interests of the rich or the skilled, unwittingly harming their own economic interests in the long term (*CW*, vol. XIX, p. 349). A conformist majority might oppress dissenting minorities or eccentric individuals. A majority of mediocre persons might elect mediocrities. In an electoral system like the British, many might effectively be disfranchised because they stood no chance of electing an MP whose views coincided with their own.

The remedy Mill favoured for these problems was proportional representation, as proposed by Thomas Hare in his *Treatise on the Election of Representatives* of 1859. Hare's scheme was excessively complex, but simpler methods could achieve its general aims. The elector would be able to choose from a list of candidates embracing a wide range of opinions. His vote would count, not only in the constituency in which he lived, but nationwide, so that quite small minorities could club their votes together to elect an MP to their taste. Mill thought that under such a system, outstanding individuals and intellectuals with a national reputation would be elected and would counterbalance the mediocrities from the localities. The majority of MPs representing class interests would be forced to defend their proposals against the arguments of the representatives of intellect and Mill, optimistically and on the basis of no evidence, thought that the better argument would often prevail (*CW*, vol. XIX, p. 458). Mill also thought that Hare's scheme would immediately work in favour of the working-class elector, and would ultimately make it unnecessary to give extra votes to the more educated (*CW*, vol. XXVIII, p. 185; vol. XIX, p. 364).

Still there was a danger that democracy would put too much power into the hands of the mediocre and ill-educated. Therefore Mill thought that a large part of the business of government should be carried out by professional experts, by a permanent, unelected civil service selected by competitive examination (*CW*, vol. XXX, pp. 38–9; vol. XIX, p. 529). Not only should the executive part of government be in their hands: Mill thought that more of the process of legislation should be done by experts. As early as 1834 he declared that laws should be drafted by a legislative commission (*CW*, vol. VI, p. 160). In Britain today, government bills are drafted by civil servants. But, in addition, Mill thought that parliament should only have the power to approve or reject their proposals *in toto*, not to make changes. Detailed meddling by ignorant amateurs representing special interests produced bad laws. To a considerable extent Mill wished to restrict parliament to a negative and checking function, able to throw out and replace a government which had abused its trust or lost contact with the sense of the nation (*CW*, vol. XIX, pp. 428–32).

To sum up so far: no votes for the uneducated or for the recipients of welfare; extra votes for the better educated; a system of proportional representation partly intended to give weight to higher intellects, and an allocation of the functions of government so as to put more into the hands of experts – it is plain that Mill, if he is a democrat, is also by twentieth-century standards élitist. In reinforcement of this verdict we might adduce his metropolitan suspicion of local government: 'Any despotism is preferable to local despotism. ... to be the slave of the vulgar prejudices, the cramped, distorted, and short-sighted views, of the public of a small town or a group of villages' (*CW*, vol. XIX, pp. 538, 606). In conclusion to this part of the discussion we might underscore Mill's decided preference, from his days of youthful Benthamism onwards, for *representative* democracy, rather than direct democracy or the election of mandated delegates: assuming that the elected are of higher calibre than their electors, the system of representation is a protection against ignorance and stupidity (*CW*, vol. XXVI, p. 367).

The spotlight has so far been turned on Mill the 'élitist' and dubious democrat. It is interesting that this side of his political thought is entirely based upon those fundamental principles he shared with his father and Bentham, concerned with protecting interests and securing efficiency. There is a more radical aspect (Ryan, 1974, p. 191) but this is less 'Benthamite', having affinities with the thought of Rousseau (1712–78), with the 'classical republican' idea of virtue embodied in independence and citizenship and the German/romantic conception of *Bildung* or personal development. For the merit of a set of political institutions consists also 'of the degree in which they promote the general mental advancement of the community, including under that phrase advancement in intellect, in virtue, and in practical activity and efficiency' (*CW*, vol. XIX, p. 392). Mill thought that the possession and use of the vote would be a factor in mental and moral improvement. The voter would be impelled to rise out of the rut of petty concerns to think about public issues. 'Wherever the sphere of action of human beings is artificially circumscribed, their sentiments are narrowed and dwarfed in the same proportion. ... Let a person have nothing to do for his country, and he will not care for it' (*CW*, vol. XIX, pp. 400–1). The converse of this was that the apathetic have no moral right to vote (*CW*, vol. XIX, pp. 338–9).

This concern to elevate the mental and moral character of the people through political involvement also finds expression in Mill's repudiation of the secret ballot. By no later than 1853 he had come to think it would be retrograde, and he openly repudiated it in 1859 (*CW*, vol. XIV, p. 103). This put him at odds with radical allies such as Grote, though Mill pointed out that his father in his *History of British India* had thought it necessary only under certain circumstances (*CW*, vol. XIX, p. 331). For a century or more the secret ballot has been associated with progress and therefore it is natural to suppose his stance to be at best quirky and at worst reactionary. But this is a mistake. Contemporary radicals may have favoured the secret ballot, but usually in the context of universal (manhood) suffrage. As long as the suffrage was restricted, an open ballot allowed the non-electors to observe and influence the electors. Mill thought that even under universal suffrage, each elector should publicly declare his or her vote. For the vote was not a right, to be used selfishly: it was a trust, to be used in the public interest, and therefore the public was entitled to know how it was being used. The voter should be shamed out of using the vote in a narrowly self-interested fashion. Publicity and criticism would encourage public spirit, and the advantages of this outweighed the dangers of bribery. Furthermore, the secret ballot would encourage lying about the vote, and 'when people have only a few of the moral feelings they ought to have, there is the more danger in weakening those few' (*CW*, vol. XXV, pp. 1214–16; vol. XIX, pp. 489–91).

The obvious criticism is to point to examples from all round the world of the intimidation of voters, by governments and parties having no inhibitions against the use of violence in elections. But Mill justifies the open ballot in the more advanced states of modern Europe on the grounds that the power of coercing voters has declined and is declining (*CW*, vol. XIX, p. 491). This is to imply that open balloting, though preferable, is only desirable where the threat of coercion is absent. Mill's stance on this question is not obviously wrong or reactionary. His concern to encourage citizens to use their votes in a responsible, public-spirited way, coupled with his plan to ensure through a system of proportional representation that every voice is heard and taken into account, brings him towards Rousseau's ideal of a general will which represents principled opinions rather than selfish interests, or the contemporary German philosopher Habermas's idea of a public consensus (*CW*, vol. XIX, p. 358).

There is another way in which his theory of democracy moves in a radical direction. In spite of his disparaging remarks about local government and the mediocrity of the people it attracts, Mill favours the extension of it, with considerable popular participation: as Tocqueville had taught him, local bodies are essential to liberty (*CW*, vol. XXX, pp. 175–6). He is in large part an opponent of centralization or, rather, he favours as much local administration as possible, watched, advised and supervised by the more intelligent centre (*CW*, vol. XIX, p. 544). This was the pattern for the New Poor Law: Mill thought that it should be applied to education too (*CW*, vol. XXIX, p. 395). In 1835 we find him writing in favour of provincial assemblies (*CW*, vol. XVIII, p. 37). Local government, local boards and jury service train 'many men of no great ability or reach of thought to be quite capable of discharging important public functions & of watching & controlling their discharge by others' (*CW*, vol. XVII, p. 1557). In addition, it must not be forgotten that Mill looks forward to democratic control of the workplace, as workers' co-operatives become more common. There is a parallel in his attitudes to India. Whereas James Mill (and later Fitzjames Stephen) thought that Indians should be passive recipients of enlightened British government, John Stuart Mill advocated the involvement of native Indians in administration because this would educate and improve them (Zastoupil, 1994, pp. 87, 204–5).

In assessing Mill's credentials as a democrat, we must be sensitive to the differences between then and now. Today, democracy is routine, taken for granted. Questions have become closed which were open in Mill's day. This does not mean that our answers are right; it means that we no longer pose the questions. His answers are not as eccentric as they seem when ripped out of the context of their time; there was considerable common ground between him and the progressive 'university liberals' (Kent, 1978). When Mill wrote, there were few democracies in the world, and limited experience of democracy. It still made sense, even for a democrat, to ask whether all should have the vote without exceptions, and whether each person should have just one vote. It was an open question whether the vote was a right or a responsibility, and whether voting should be open or secret. Bearing this in mind, paying attention to both the élitist and radical strands in Mill's writings, and recognizing that democracy is not a Platonic essence but a contested concept, it seems right to accept Mill's unvarying claim that he was a democrat.

What is more, he was a democrat in practice. When he spoke in favour of the Liberal Reform Bill of 1866, he did not advocate universal suffrage, which was not a possibility at that time. But the central

thrust of his speech was in favour of giving a political voice to the working classes. In 1837 he had written that radical MPs should 'do everything for the good of the working classes, which it would be necessary
to do if there were Universal Suffrage' (*CW*, vol. VI, p. 397). As an MP
he thought of himself as a representative of those as yet unenfran-
chised, unempowered classes. He advanced their case on trade union
legislation in 1867 and supported working-class candidates for parliament, in speeches, in writing and with money. In order to forward the
political education of the working classes he brought out his principal
works in cheap People's Editions, in some cases forgoing his royalties to
secure a lower price (*CW*, vol. XV, p. 922). He thought that the working
class should have working-class MPs; in two-member liberal constituen-
cies one should be selected by labourers. Ideally, 50 per cent of MPs
should represent wage-earners, and there ought to be working men
and women on elected School Boards (*CW*, vol. XVI, p. 1464; vol. XVII,
pp. 1542–3; vol. XXVIII, p. 30; vol. XXIX, p. 400).

Socialism

Whether Mill was a socialist has been hotly debated: rival interpretations are sketched by Kurer (who provides a good bibliography) and
Riley and will not be rehearsed here (Kurer, 1992; Riley, 1996,
pp. 39–41). Mill sat at Ricardo's feet and began as a defender of free-
market capitalism; this was his position in his debates with co-operative
socialist followers of Robert Owen (1771–1859) in 1825, when he produced some devastating arguments. He began to move towards socialism in the 1830s under the influence of Saint-Simonianism and the
communitarian socialism of Fourier (1772–1837), the latter mediated
and brought down to earth for him by Considérant (1808–93). He
thought Fourierism more realistic than Owenism: it did not require the
members of its communities to be perfect altruists, and was prepared to
give extra rewards to capital, talent and effort. The critical evolution
came between 1847 and 1852, as he completed and brought out the
first three editions of the *Principles of Political Economy*, progressively
moving towards a more favourable evaluation of socialism. Their correspondence proves that Harriet egged him on, sometimes persuading
him to be less cautious than he wished (Hayek, 1951, pp. 133–9): his
reluctance to make assertions without proof has frequently been noted
in this book and he thought a conclusive decision between socialism

and an ideal régime of private property would not be possible until both had been tried. But his admiration for the co-operative experiments in France before and during the 1848 revolution also pushed him in the same direction. In the last four years of his life he wrote 'Our ideal of ultimate improvement...would class us decidedly under the general designation of Socialists' (*CW*, vol. 1, p. 239) and nowhere in the *Autobiography* is this retracted. Some have thought that a retraction is signalled in the posthumously published *Chapters on Socialism*, but the evidently incomplete nature of that work makes any such inference unsound.

So why, if Mill called himself a socialist, has that description been contested? The answer is that 'socialism' is not a timeless Platonic idea but rather a handy term covering several different theories and practical proposals. We need to be clear which of these Mill agreed with. In the first place, Mill's socialism was different from that of Marx. Of course there were similarities. Like Marx, he had a vivid sense of class conflict in industrial society. His critique of capitalism occasionally exhibited a 'Marxist' ferocity: he thought that the existing capitalist order enslaved the labourers, and recognized that wealth does not flow to those who create it (*CW*, vol. II, pp. 207–9; vol. III, p. 767). But, unlike Marx, he was utterly opposed to any total and revolutionary transformation of society in one go. This would be anarchy, this would be chaos come again, out of which no good could arise (*CW*, vol. V, pp. 709, 749). Mill was not a man of violence and thought that if the state took a person's property, it should pay full compensation.

Neither was Mill a state socialist of the Fabian or of any other kind. This was made manifest in his arguments against Saint-Simonism, whose supporters proposed a society centrally managed by experts (*CW*, vol. XVII, pp. 1609–10). Mill thought this would be an intolerable tyranny; the people at large would not accept it. It would be inefficient too; a central committee could never match the detailed local knowledge of private individuals. In spite of the fact that he was a public servant, Mill had little faith in the honesty and diligence of paid officials unchecked by a representative body. Nor was he a 'welfare socialist'. He had no time for the idea that ordinary people should be paternalistically looked after: they should learn to look after themselves. He expects citizens to buy private education wherever possible, and to provide for sickness and old age by means of private insurance (under certain conditions he would not rule out compulsory, universal insurance – *CW*, vol. XVI, p. 1390). Where this fails, and for the unemployed, Mill remained throughout his life a defender of the principles of the New Poor Law of 1834 – though he came to condemn some of the harsher features of its actual working. In 1848 he thought it impossible to separate the deserving poor from the able-bodied on whom the rigours of the workhouse should fall with full weight: by 1868 he was lamenting that Chadwick's original plan to separate off the sick, the lunatic, the old and the young and to give them better treatment had not been implemented (*CW*, vol. XXXII, p. 75; vol. XVI, pp. 1431–2; vol. XXVIII p. 358). So Mill was at odds with the forms of socialism, both Marxist and social democratic, which prevailed in the century following his death. This largely explains the incredulity of so many commentators towards his declaration of socialist allegiance.

But if he is compared with the Utopian Socialists of the 1830s and 1840s, and with the Christian Socialists and co-operators of the mid-nineteenth century, his designation as a socialist is less problematic. Utopian Socialism repudiated the selfish individualism of 'economic man' as conceived by classical political economy. It was a high moral ideal based on altruism and community, and it was this that appealed to Mill and Harriet. Mill differed from the Owenites (and to some extent from Harriet) in thinking that it would take many generations to educate the mass of the people for unselfishness. Socialism was a long way off. He also differed from most Utopians (in spite of Kurer's argument – Kurer, 1992, pp. 227–8) in thinking that competition was beneficial, and that it would be needed for a long time, perhaps indefinitely. Competition was a vital incentive to hard work and efficiency. Mill persisted in defending competitive markets: and to some this is enough to rule him out as a socialist. But perhaps what he most resembles is a late twentieth-century 'market socialist', who advocates a mix of enterprises – owned by the state, by municipalities, by capitalists and by workers' co-operatives – competing in the market place.

Mill was not thinking of Owenite co-operative communities; he had objections on economic grounds and opposed any kind of 'communism' because of the threat it posed to liberty. He favoured more modest producers' and consumers' co-operatives. He claimed in 1865 to have advocated these five years before the Rochdale pioneers of 1844, whose co-operative store inspired the Co-operative movement (*CW*, vol. XVIII, p. 29). In fact, he first recommended producers' co-operatives in 1834 (*CW*, vol. VI, p. 190). In the second edition of the

Principles of Political Economy he introduced the idea that the form of association of the future was

> not that which can exist between a capitalist as chief, and workpeople without a voice in the management, but the association of the labourers themselves on terms of equality, collectively owning the capital with which they carry on their operations, and working under managers elected and removable by themselves (*CW*, vol. II, p. 775).

In the future, only the least improved workpeople would consent to work for wages. This is the kernel and essence of Mill's socialism, and it *is* socialism: Mill was emphatic that all who work in a co-operative should be shareholders and that there should be no labourers merely for hire: 'It is not genuine co-operation, where any of the co-operators are excluded from the division of the whole produce'. Workers should pool their savings in order to set up co-operatives, and should also borrow on the open market. Mill had no objections to money lent at interest: he thought that the base rate of 3 per cent in his own day would go lower, and 'who can say that this is too much, or that it is unreasonable for the use of capital to be applied for the purposes of labour?' (*CW*, vol. XVIII, pp. 6–7). This would not be capital hiring labour, but labour hiring capital (*CW*, vol. V, p. 412).

Mill envisages a role for capitalist employers for many years to come. First, co-operation is suited to improved, educated, public-spirited labourers; lazy and vicious workers need a boss. Second, owner management is efficient and enterprising, because the capitalist receives the fruits of success and pays the penalty for failure. Co-operative management might be cautious, routine; democratically accountable managers would be less able to take risks (*CW*, vol. V, pp. 739–41). If private capitalist firms can interest their employees in the success of the enterprise by profit-sharing, they will have well-motivated workers and management, and will survive well in competition with co-operatives (*CW*, vol. III, pp. 792–3). Mill's defence of workers' co-ops rests upon ideals of democracy and independence and upon a desire to promote unselfish motivations, as much as or more than on considerations of efficiency.

Mill's prophecy that co-operatives would eventually prevail have not been realized, and there are many reasons for this. The growing and now multinational scale of corporations is no help, nor is the shortage of producers' co-operatives as a model and inspiration.

Perhaps a capitalist environment is hostile to co-operative experiments; Mill had reason to know this. In 1865 he sent a donation of £10 to the Wolverhampton Platelock Makers' Co-operative. It had been founded in 1864, but now the capitalist employers were trying to ruin it by selling platelocks below cost. 'In such a contest', Mill wrote, 'if prolonged, the competitors who have the smallest means, though they may have every other element of success, must necessarily be crushed through no fault of their own' (*CW*, vol. XVI, p. 1020).

No account of Mill's socialism is complete without reference to his views on land. In the *Principles of Political Economy* he denied any absolute right of private property in land: no man made it and it remained a common heritage of the people. We have seen that he recommended state action to create peasant proprietors in Ireland. As a member of the Land Tenure Reform Association in the 1870s he was recommending that the state purchase land on the open market in order to create small farms or large co-operative ones. A year before his death he hinted in private at the eventual possibility of the resumption of all land by the state, with compensation to the landholders (*CW*, vol. XVII, p. 1899).

Some related issues now require consideration: distribution, taxation and the scope of state activity. In 1869 came his 'recantation' of the wages fund theory, in the second part of his review of his former India House colleague Thornton's *On Labour and its Claims*. This has puzzled some economists, who have doubted whether Mill really changed his mind (Hollander, 1985, pp. 393–419). The truth of the matter is that there was no sudden conversion: Mill's position gradually evolved. By 1869 he did not think that there was a fixed wages fund, so that if some workers got more by striking others would inevitably get less. He recognized that although the level of wages was in some ultimate way determined by the relationship between supply and demand in the market – between the number of workers seeking work, and the number of jobs on offer – nevertheless workers would often not get the market rate unless they organized themselves in trade unions and threatened strike action. Because the initiative lay with the employer, who offered work at a certain wage, wages tended to be lower than they would be if workers initiated the bargain. The wage fund was elastic: workers could get more without harming other workers if they compelled their employers to forfeit some of the profits they would have spent on a lavish lifestyle. But this elasticity was limited. The supply of capital was finite and excessive wage rises would harm investment: to this extent the wages fund theory remained true. Mill therefore accorded a role to trade unions in securing a more equitable distribution of wealth.

But he was no unqualified defender of trade union activity. He disapproved of the stand of the Amalgamated Society of Engineers in 1852 against piecework and overtime, and penned some harsh remarks on this subject in the essay *On Liberty*: 'It is known that the bad workmen who form the majority … in many branches of industry, are decidedly of the opinion that bad workmen ought to receive the same wages as good' (*CW*, vol. XVIII, p. 287). Not only did Mill favour piecework: he also believed in performance-related pay as an incentive to hard work and efficiency: 'The teacher's duty [may] be idly and inefficiently performed if his remuneration is certain … But where is the necessity that the teacher's pay should bear no relation to the number and proficiency of his pupils?' (*CW*, vol. V, p. 624).

Mill's thoughts on taxation were subtle, complex, and evolving throughout his life: only the main lines can be sketched here. He aimed to combine fairness (interpreted as equality of sacrifice) with cheapness of collection, the promotion of economic growth and redistribution in the interests of greater equality. An ideal system would combine direct and indirect taxes. An income tax was justifiable in an emergency, when an exceptionally large sum had to be raised. But it should not be levied on the basic income required to purchase 'what is necessary for healthful existence', by which Mill meant something more generous than just enough to stave off starvation (*CW*, vol. III, p. 830; vol. V, p. 497). Above that level it should be flat rate; higher rates on higher incomes are unjust, because they penalize hard work and thrift (*CW*, vol. III, pp. 810–11). But in normal times he did not favour an income tax, because it is too easy to evade. It is a tax paid by the conscientious and avoided by the unscrupulous: a tax on honesty (*CW*, vol. III, p. 832).

Mill thought that a house tax, a rate, was a better direct tax; if proportioned to the value of the house it tended to correspond to income and could not be evaded. But basic housing should be exempt 'on the universal principle of sparing from all taxation the absolute necessaries of healthful existence' (*CW*, vol. III, p. 837). He also favoured a hefty land tax. As explained in Chapter 3, Ricardian theory explained rent as an unearned increment, which increased with economic growth without any effort on the part of the landlord. Mill hoped that this unearned increment 'will be gradually, and in an increasing proportion, diverted from them to the nation as a whole, from whose collective exertions and sacrifices it really proceeds' (*CW*, vol. V, p. 691). This is in embryo the Fabian socialist theory of taxation, as developed in the 1880s.

In the *Principles of Political Economy* he proposed a further attack on unearned wealth in the form of heavy inheritance taxes, and thought that this 'would pull down all large fortunes in two generations' (Bain, 1882, p. 89). He recognized a right of bequest, but severely limited the right of inheritance, thinking that no-one has a right to be rich without effort. The fortunes of those who die intestate, if they have no ascending or descending heirs (parents, children, etc.), should go to the state. Collaterals (brothers, cousins, etc.) should have no right of inheritance. The children of those who die intestate should receive no more than will suffice to complete their education or training for self-sufficiency, or no more than would give them a comfortable existence. They should not receive enough to keep a spouse and children in comfort. Where there is a will, Mill proposes that there should be a limit on what any individual may inherit.

> Each person should have power to dispose by will of his or her whole property; but not to lavish it in enriching some one individual, beyond a certain maximum, which should be fixed sufficiently high to afford the means of comfortable independence (*CW*, vol. II, p. 225).

But what exactly is a 'comfortable independence'? This looks like a wealthy leisured class. It is reminiscent of the 'clerisy' proposed by Coleridge and echoed by Mill, a class of persons having the leisure to read, think and write. He would also allow some to inherit more, where it would make economic sense to keep a business intact in the hands of one heir, or where an individual inherits the responsibility for keeping up an ancestral mansion and park or pleasure ground (*CW*, vol. II, p. 225). Some recent commentators have thought that Mill was a radical egalitarian (Donner, 1991, p. 159), others that his proposals were only minimally redistributive (Kurer, 1991b, pp. 713–14, 721). But by 1871 he favoured a heavy graduated inheritance tax which would compel all to work (*CW*, vol. XVII, p. 1848). Here is further evidence of Mill's increasing radicalism in his final years.

Where indirect taxes are concerned, Mill continues to insist on the principle of exempting the poor. The necessities of a healthful existence should pay no tax; indirect taxes should fall on comforts only. Mill was reluctant to single out 'luxuries' for higher taxation: 'I do not think a distinction can be fairly made between comforts and luxuries,

or that I am entitled to call my tea and coffee by the one name, and
another person's melons and champagne by the other' (*CW*, vol. XV,
p. 976). But he did want to distinguish comforts and luxuries from
mere status goods, such as jewellery or expensive carriages, which were
especially suitable for taxation (*CW*, vol. III, pp. 868–72).

Mill's desire to limit the role of the state, forcibly expressed in
Book V of his *Principles of Political Economy* and in the essay *On Liberty*,
is well known. In the former he writes that '*Laisser-faire*, in short, should
be the general practice: every departure from it, unless required by
some great good, is a certain evil' (*CW*, vol. III, p. 945). In *On Liberty*
he insists that if all large enterprises were branches of government,
'not all the freedom of the press and popular constitution of the
legislature would make this or any other country free otherwise than
in name' (*CW*, vol. XVIII, p. 306). It is best to leave individuals to
manage their own affairs; they will usually do it more efficiently
than the state could, and self-management will be good for personal
development.

It would, however, be a mistake to think that Mill was in favour of a
minimal state: he thought that Herbert Spencer was far too hostile to
government agency (*CW*, vol. XV, p. 888). His general assertion of
laisser-faire is curiously qualified by a considerable list of instances
where state action is appropriate. Those who, like Dicey, thought that
Mill's philosophy anticipated twentieth-century collectivism were not
entirely wrong. State intervention is appropriate in cases of market
failure; he thought that there was nothing which free trade did
absolutely well (*CW*, vol. V, p. 622). Where private interests cannot be
relied upon to pay for public goods, such as lighthouses or scientific
research, government should step in. Education is a similar case of the
utmost importance. Most parents have neither the motivation nor the
knowledge to impel them to purchase in the marketplace an education
suited to their children's interests and to the needs of society; therefore
the state must intervene. But the kind of intervention Mill proposes is
significant. The state may compel parents to have their children educated, and may even pay for that education if they are poor; but it
should not be the universal provider. Private providers are best, for
they allow for diversity and freedom of thought: a state system could
become a system of indoctrination in approved values. There should be
universal public examinations to ensure that all children attain certain
standards whether educated privately or by the state: but 'All attempts
by the State to bias the conclusions of its citizens on disputed subjects,

are evil' (*CW*, vol. XVIII, p. 303). Mill, it is clear, would have detested the national curriculum.

He was not averse to measures of nationalization or municipalization; natural monopolies such as gas and water or railways could appropriately come into public ownership. He did not object to the provision of services by the state, if that was the only or most efficient way of doing it. For example, he favoured a state monopoly of the postal services (*CW*, vol. III, p. 860). There could be municipal provision of gardens, theatres, galleries, baths and housing and state ownership of natural beauties and historic monuments (*CW*, vol. V, pp. 213–14; vol. XV, p. 609; vol. XVI, pp. 1155–6; vol. XVII, p. 1741). But public ownership need not imply state management; almost always the state would do better to hire a private agency to run a nationalized industry (*CW*, vol. III, p. 956).

A pattern of values underlies Mill's socioeconomic vision. He favoured liberty, and was not prepared to contemplate any form of socialism which threatened it: but did not think that liberty equated to the capitalist free market. He favoured independence, and consequently was suspicious of paternalistic welfare. He favoured self-government to such an extent as to think that master–servant, employer–employee relationships were unsound and to hope for their eventual supersession. He favoured equality: 'I look upon inequality as *in itself* always an evil' (*CW*, vol. XVII, p. 2002), but not at the expense of efficiency, nor if it penalized effort and saving. He had no time for unearned, unmerited advantages, and was utterly committed to equality of opportunity. His account of what was needed to secure the latter is inadequate by modern standards, but he thought that primary education should be compulsory for all, and free secondary and higher education provided for the élite of the poor (*CW*, vol. V, pp. 627–8). He unreservedly supported the opening of the civil service to competitive examination, brusquely dismissing the suggestion that a horse-dealer's son was unsuitable, and that gentlemen could not be expected to mix with one (*CW*, vol. XXX, pp. 38–9).

Feminism

Mill was at least an incipient feminist before he met Harriet Taylor in 1830, and his background had prepared him for it. His father rejected votes for women in his *Essay on Government*, but Bentham favoured them.

James Mill may have treated his wife as a 'squah', but Mill's sisters studied a tough curriculum alongside their brothers (*CW*, vol. XII, p. 10).
In the 1820s Mill knew and respected the Owenite socialist feminist
William Thompson. Then, in the early 1830s, feminist influences
streamed in on him from Harriet Taylor, from the Unitarian circle
around the *Monthly Repository* to which she belonged, and from Saint-
Simonian and Fourierist socialism. His feminism evolved and deep-
ened. In the mid-1820s we find him, under the influence of the
eighteenth-century philosophical historian John Millar, writing in the
spirit of the Scottish Enlightenment: savages and barbarians treat
women brutally, their good treatment is a mark of high civilization.
In the seraglio and in modern Europe they are used 'as trinkets worn
for display … shutting them up like jewels in a case' (*CW*, vol. XX,
pp. 45–6). In the early 1830s, he and Harriet exchanged letters setting
out their views of marriage, and Mill's letter mingled the radical
with the conventional and sentimental: 'her occupation should rather
be to adorn and beautify … that will be her natural task, if task it can
be called which will in so great a measure, be accomplished rather
by *being* than by *doing*' (*CW*, vol. XXI, p. 43). Harriet's letter is perfectly unsentimental and robust, and Mill largely gave up such senti-
mentalities – in this matter Harriet was no doubt a good influence
who progressively raised his consciousness. In 1832, he wrote in favour
of banning women from factory work by law, so as not to take
them away from their families. Some Lancashire women objected, and
he conceded that 'the interdiction might be confined to *married*
females, and those whose parents are alive and not in the receipt of
parish relief' (*CW*, vol. XXIII, pp. 398–401, 419–20). But by the time
of the *Principles of Political Economy* of 1848 he was resolutely opposed
to paternalistic treatment of women as if they were children
(*CW*, vol. III, p. 953). As early as 1834 we find him objecting to the use
of masculine terms to refer to all humans, and by the time he came
to reprint his essays in 1859 he was systematically replacing 'he'
and 'his' with 'they' and 'their' (*CW*, vol. XXIII, p. 729n). He opposed
sentimental, vulgar and essentializing talk about 'woman' instead
of 'women' (*CW*, vol. XV, p. 510). In the 1840s and 1850s came the
series of articles highlighting men's violence against women, and in
1867 he moved his amendment to the Parliamentary Reform Bill with
the aim of giving votes to women on the same terms as men.
In 1869 he published his feminist classic, which had been drafted
about 1860.

Mill's essay on *The Subjection of Women* divides into four sections. In the first he reflects on the belief that women should be subordinate to men, exposing it as an unfounded prejudice and explaining why the prejudice is so deeply entrenched. In the second he examines the unequal laws relating to marriage, in the third the exclusion of women from various employments, and in the fourth he sets out the benefits which would flow from according women freedom and equality. The book is a classic repertory of good arguments against discrimination.

Mill's piecemeal demolition of the case against women is sustained by four fundamental lines of argument. First, the associationist or environmentalist one that apparent differences between the 'nature' of women and the 'nature' of men may not be natural at all, but wholly artificial, generated by environment, conditioning and education. We do not know what women in general are capable of, because they have rarely been given the chance to show their mettle. No-one has expressed this classic feminist argument more eloquently (*CW*, vol. XXI, pp. 276–7).

A second structural argument of the book relates the subjection of women to a historical grand narrative leading to the conclusion that the emancipation of women is both likely and morally imperative. Primitive social relations were governed by brutality, force, the law of the strongest; as civilization has advanced, brute force has given way to humanity, reason, justice and freedom. Slaves have been emancipated, serfs and burgesses freed from the oppression of feudal lords, nations have shaken off the yoke of absolute monarchs. Relations between men and women are the only area where the law of the strongest prevails, and this is 'the primitive state of slavery lasting on. ... It has not lost the taint of its brutal origin.' 'There remain no legal slaves, except the mistress of every house' (*CW*, vol. XXI, pp. 264, 323).

The historical construction is reinforced by a social and psychological one; Mill emphasizes the plight of women who are married to the lowest dregs of the population, to men little better than animals; they may be subjected to beating, marital rape and even murder. The extremity of his language – 'vilest malefactor', 'atrocity', 'mean and savage natures', 'victim' and 'executioner', 'absolute monsters', 'animalism and selfishness', 'ferocious savages' – demonstrates the depth of his concern (*CW*, vol. XXI, pp. 287–8). By this rhetorical strategy he who would put women into subjection is associated with the stage which history has left behind, with the savage and the criminal, with social trash and with those whose higher natures have been overwhelmed by their lower and animal ones.

A third major theme is the ideal of companionship in marriage (Shanley, 1991, pp. 172–3). No doubt there have always been examples of it, and the ideal in a recognizably modern form goes back to sixteenth-century puritanism if not earlier. But Mill is right in thinking that the ideal had become more prevalent and influential, as men's lives became more domestic and as they spent their leisure with their wives rather than in 'the rough amusements and convivial excesses which formerly occupied most men in their hours of relaxation'. He is right too when he argues that true friendship in marriage is almost impossible where the partners are very different in tastes and character, completely impossible when their relationship is that of superior to inferior. His sentences glow with enthusiasm for a marriage between two cultivated equals, identical in opinions and purposes. Undoubtedly he has his own union with Harriet Taylor in mind, and, as a dark contrast and warning, the decidedly uncompanionate marriage of his own parents (*CW*, vol. XXI, pp. 335–6).

Finally, Mill accumulates a series of utilitarian arguments for the emancipation of women, showing that society will benefit. There are never enough able people to do the world's work, and excluding women from higher employments halves the pool of talent (*CW*, vol. XXI, p. 326). Then there are several ways in which the emancipation of women will benefit men. Men's characters are corrupted when society accords them a superiority over others which they have not merited, when every man, no matter how inadequate, can fancy himself superior to every member of the opposite sex. For Mill this is an exact parallel with the unearned status and power of aristocracy which also, in his view, corrupts and enervates; he is committed to the invigorating effects of meritocracy, of which female emancipation is a necessary part.

Not only does the subjection of women corrupt men by ascribing them unmerited status and thereby weakening their sense of justice; it also encourages them in habits of tyranny and domination. Furthermore, companionship in marriage produces ill effects when combined with sex inequality. A man who spends his time with an uncultivated, ill-informed woman insensibly adjusts to his company and slowly degenerates; 'If the wife does not push the husband forward, she always holds him back' (*CW*, vol. XXI, p. 335). Women can have great influence for good; because of their physical weakness, for instance, they discourage violence and promote the humanizing effects of civilization. But if this softening influence is combined with a lack of education, it can do harm. Women engage in works of charity: but if they do not understand the principles of political economy, the money they dole out to the poor may entrench poverty rather than relieving it (*CW*, vol. XXI, pp. 330–1). Finally, the uneducated wife holds back the fearless radical man who would otherwise stand up for his principles in spite of society's disapproval. She cannot appreciate his courage and commitment to principles because she cannot understand them; all she sees is the loss of social status to herself, and of job and marriage opportunities to her children. Her influence is all in the direction of mediocrity and respectability. 'Whoever has a wife and children has given hostages to Mrs Grundy' (*CW*, vol. XXI, p. 332). (Mrs Grundy was a censorious character in a play of 1800.)

No-one today denies the importance of Mill's *The Subjection of Women*, or that he was a noble and inspiring precursor of modern feminism. But the essay has been subjected to feminist criticism. Doubts have been expressed about the discussion in Chapter 3 of the aptitudes of women and their suitability to various occupations and activities. Mill prefaces his argument with a restatement of his environmentalist credo, and provides a classic explanation of why women have displayed so little in the way of original genius in the sciences and the arts: it has nothing to do with a lack of ability and everything to do with a lack of opportunity and encouragement. A minor criticism here is that he underestimates the extent of female achievement in the arts and fails to recognize the way in which excellence has been defined in terms of what men do.

But then he runs the risk of bringing natural difference, and natural inferiority, back in. For he considers the mental differences between men and women *as they presently appear*, in order to make out a case for the 'peculiar tendencies and aptitudes characteristic of women'. Women have more rapid insight into character; they tend to be better than men at practice (as contrasted with theory); they are more down to earth and realistic, and sensitive to the needs of individuals; they think and judge more quickly; they are capable of greater spirit and enthusiasm; their minds are more mobile and flexible (*CW*, vol. XXI, pp. 302–10). To the critic this sells the pass to the anti-feminist enemy. The oldest trick in the patriarchalist book is to praise women for their special talents, and then to infer that those talents perfectly equip them to complement (and serve) men and to assume their role in a separate (and inferior) sphere. For the differences Mill emphasizes resemble the clichéd contrast between male logic and female intuition. He even hazards the suggestion that these perceived differences may be related to differences in brain size and structure. If women's brains are smaller, then they may be better adapted to speed of response and flexibility, to doing several things at once or in quick succession; if men's brains are larger, then perhaps they will bear more heavy work, single-mindedly grinding slowly and steadily away at problems until they are solved (*CW*, vol. XXI, pp. 311–12).

But if the text is read carefully and sympathetically, the worst that can be said about Mill's argument is that he has chosen an unfortunate rhetorical strategy. He has decided to give his opponent the benefit of the doubt, and to assume for the sake of argument that the differences which appear between men and women really are essential differences. Mill thus, as it were, goes into the fray with one hand tied behind his back. But, he can now say, even though my opponent has been allowed to choose his own ground, even though I have given up, for the time being, some of my best arguments, nevertheless I can show that the traditionally accepted characteristics of women fit them to take on executive tasks and to be managers and rulers. This may have seemed a clever argument to Mill: but perhaps he made a dangerous concession to his opponent, and one which can all too easily be turned against him.

Putting the best case for Mill, he *never* concludes that there are essential differences of character, aptitude and ability between men and women: 'I shall presently show, that even the least contestable of the differences which now exist, are such as may very well have been produced merely by circumstances, without any difference of natural capacity' (*CW*, vol. XXI, p. 305). From writings at different times in his life it is clear that Mill had a persistent and rooted dislike of commonplace and essentializing distinctions between 'masculinity' and 'femininity'. But in his careful formulations he avoids the opposite position of asserting categorically that there are *no* essential differences. True to the scientific stance we saw manifested in the *Logic*, he resolutely refuses to draw conclusions beyond what the evidence will bear. In his day, the relevant sciences were not sufficiently developed to provide firm answers (nor are they at the end of the twentieth century); the relationship between the physical structure of the brain and its intellectual powers was a subject of dispute, and the laws of the formation of character (the science which Mill called 'ethology'), had been little studied (*CW*, vol. XXI, p. 312). Finally, in Mill's defence it should be pointed out that present-day feminists are by no means united over whether to insist upon special female/feminine characteristics (whether natural or cultural) or not. There has been a reaction against the 'equality feminism' of, for example, Wollstonecraft (1759–97) and de Beauvoir (1908–86), according to which women's minds can and should be just like men's, and there is now a tendency to celebrate difference (Gilligan, 1982). 'Difference feminists' might be less inclined to criticize Mill for saying that women were more likely to favour compromise than conflict, that their enfranchisement would strengthen the influences opposed to violence and bloodshed, and that they would be more likely to protect natural beauty (*CW*, vol. XVI, p. 1442; vol. XVII, pp. 1659, 1838). They might welcome Donner's finding of a 'feminist' ethic of caring in Mill's concern for the culture of the feelings (Donner, 1993, pp. 156–7).

From a twentieth-century point of view it is less easy to defend Mill's role prescriptions for married women. He thought that gainful employments should be opened up to women in equal competition with men, and women should receive the education necessary to make that competition fair. For this is essential to a woman's dignity; it raises her value in the eyes of her husband. But 'like a man when he chooses a profession, so, when a woman marries, it may in general be understood that she makes choice of the management of a household, and the bringing up of a family, as the first call upon her exertions' (*CW*, vol. XXI, p. 298). Here, separate spheres are firmly back in place: to a radical feminist, this shows up the limitations of Mill's 'liberal feminism' which fails to recognize that the patriarchal household is the prime site of women's oppression. In mitigation it might be remarked that Mill's recommendation is a qualified one: he insists that individual circumstances should be allowed to vary the rule, that for example talented women should not be precluded by marriage from pursuing vocations. He intends also that women should have careers before they have children and after their children have grown up. And it can be said that scarcely any late nineteenth-century feminists envisaged the two-career family and shared parenting. Given the magnitude of the task of running a household, with few labour-saving devices, this is hardly surprising. Offen reminds us that the dominant form of feminism in nineteenth-century Europe was a 'relational' feminism, emphasizing motherhood and companionate, non-hierarchical marriage (Offen, 1988, pp.135–6). To an extent it would be anachronistic to expect Mill to think other than he did.

But only to an extent: for his wife was perfectly capable of adopting and expressing a more 'advanced' stance. In the exchange of letters on marriage in the 1830s mentioned earlier, Mill wrote that 'It does not follow that a woman should *actually* support herself because she should be *capable* of doing so ... it is not desirable to burthen the labour market with a double number of competitors'. Harriet floats the idea of abolishing marriage entirely, opening up all occupations to women so that they would no longer have to 'barter person for bread', and making fathers and mothers equally responsible for the economic support of children (*CW*, vol. XXI, pp. 376–7). In her essay on 'The Enfranchisement of Women' of 1851 she rejects the argument that giving all women jobs would overstock the labour market, insisting that every woman must have her own earnings in order to redress the balance of power in the sexual relationship (*CW*, vol. XXI, pp. 403–4).

Mill has also been criticized for his arguments in the last chapter of the essay defending the emancipation of women because of the benefits it will bring to men. Such criticism is understandable, but inappropriate. Many late twentieth-century women feel insulted by the implication that, when they claim their rights, they need to take the further step of justifying them; after all, men are not required to justify their right to control their property and to compete for employment. But we must remember that Mill was a Utilitarian, committed to the belief that all rights require justification. And once again, his argument should be considered as a carefully chosen rhetorical strategy. Mill knows that given the existing distribution of power, *men* must be persuaded to change the law, and therefore it is sensible to show men that they have an interest in doing so. We must distinguish between the arguments which Mill uses to persuade others, and the arguments by which he himself is persuaded. It is plain from the way he concludes the essay that *he* wants to end the subjection of women for women's sake, not for men's: 'But it would be a grievous understatement of the case to omit the most direct benefit of all, the unspeakable gain in private happiness to the liberated half of the species' (*CW*, vol. XXI, p. 336). A lack of sensitivity to anachronism and rhetorical strategy is what is so wrong with Annas's hostile article, and so right with Urbinati's illuminating contextualization (Annas, 1977; Urbinati, 1991).

Mill can finally be criticized for things he does *not* say. He is rightly appalled about the practice of husbands taking their sexual pleasure whether their wives want it or not, but has little to say in criticism of the construction of sexuality in such a way as to maximize pleasure for men regardless of the pleasures of women – an issue which has been central to feminism since its revival in the 1970s. Some have thought

that he despised sexual pleasure, and that this led him to take an
unappealing view of marriage as a 'dowdy and ascetic partnership'
(Thomas, 1985, p. 122; Mendus, 1989, pp. 172, 179, 189–90). He
makes no mention of mechanical contraception, so essential if women
are to control their own bodies. He does not come out clearly and
publicly in favour of divorce, even though he was privately in favour
of 'entire freedom on both sides to dissolve this like any other partnership' (*CW*, vol. XIV, p. 500). In 1850 he had thought that the time
was not yet ripe, though in 1851 he did publish the remark that 'equality
of freedom...is the final destiny of the institution of marriage'
(*CW*, vol. V, p. 456). By the time of *The Subjection of Women* he also
thought that the issue could not properly be tackled until women had
the vote and could play an equal part in deciding it (*CW*, vol. XIV,
pp. 47–8; vol. XVII, pp. 1618, 1634, 1751). This was a sound attitude
if divorce was not to be a device whereby men could trade in wives
for younger models, leaving their former partners destitute. And in
1870 he told the Royal Commission on the Contagious Diseases Acts
that a woman should have a right to divorce if her husband gave her
a sexually transmitted disease (*CW*, vol. XXI, pp. 354–5).

Is it anachronistic to expect a respectable Victorian to be outspoken
about these issues? In part the answer must be yes; once again some
respect should be accorded to Mill's careful choice of political and
rhetorical strategy. After all, when after Mill's death Gladstone was told
about his youthful propagandizing for mechanical contraception, he
withdrew his support for a monument in Westminster Abbey. Fitzjames
Stephen found the discussion of women even as it stands in *The
Subjection of Women* slightly disgusting. But we should not assume that
it would have been *impossible* for Mill to discuss women's sexual pleasure
and artificial contraception in the 1860s; for the Owenite socialists, as
Mill knew, had been discussing these matters in the 1820s.

It can also be contended that Mill does not face up to the economic
conditions of women's emancipation. He wants to diminish the dependence of women on men, and to this end would open up all or most
professions to both sexes. But women with dependent children need
help with childcare, and guarantees that periods out of paid work will
not adversely affect their careers and earning abilities. Otherwise
they may face a stark choice between poverty and dependence on a
man. Mill fails to confront these issues, and makes matters worse by
insisting that the primary responsibility for rearing children rests with
the wife. It is not anachronistic to criticise him on this score; once

again, the Owenite socialists had already recognized these problems and proposed solutions to them. Harriet Taylor Mill hinted at their ideas in 'The Enfranchisement of Women' (*CW*, vol. XXI, p. 404). One may speculate that Mill's profound commitment to Malthusianism prevented him from considering arrangements designed to make rearing children easier.

Feminist campaigning played an important part in the last few years of Mill's life. As a member of parliament, he presented petitions and moved an amendment for women's suffrage. In 1868 he sponsored the Married Women's Property Bill. It is worth remembering that when he married Harriet Taylor in 1851, he signed a declaration renouncing the rights over her property which the law gave him. Out of parliament he was closely involved, through his stepdaughter Helen, in the work of the National Society for Women's Suffrage. Their behaviour has recently attracted some criticism; they tried to control the society, sometimes from Avignon, and to subvert those women who disagreed with them (Caine, 1978). They wanted to keep the agitation in the hands of ladylike rather than vulgar women, and thought it preferable for a speaker to be feminine or to have a pretty face (*CW*, vol. XVII, pp. 1649, 1742–5, 1851, 1918). They wanted the London Committee to break off relations with the one in Manchester, they tried to get women they disapproved of removed from the committee, and they even for a time thought such a leading campaigner as Millicent Garrett Fawcett unsound (*CW*, vol. XVI, p. 1510; vol. XVII, pp. 1835–7, 1921).

The issue was tactics. Mill was convinced that the prime necessity was the vote: once women had that, they could use their political power to tackle other oppressions. He was as opposed to the Contagious Diseases Acts as anyone, and in 1870 testified powerfully against them to the Royal Commission. But he felt that the two issues should be kept separate, for there was a danger that potential allies on the suffrage issue would be put off by so 'indelicate and unfeminine' a subject as the regulation and inspection of prostitutes (*CW*, vol. XVI, pp. 1345, 1378–9; vol. XVII, p. 1854; vol. XXIX, p. 386). From the point of view of modern and especially radical feminism this is reprehensible, typical of the failings of 'liberal' feminism which focuses on political issues rather than on the (as they see it) more fundamental oppression grounded in the sexual use and abuse of women. But there were contemporary women feminists, in addition to Mill's stepdaughter, who shared his opinions on tactics. If Mill and Helen were at once high-handed and underhand, this reflects the passion of their commitment to the cause. It is at least arguable that Mill was right, and that here again is testimony to his sense of politics as the art of the possible. Even if he was wrong, mistakes about tactics do not impugn the sincerity and wholeheartedness of his feminism.

6

CONCLUSION

Mill's place in history is assured. In the drama of events he played a significant role through his support of radical causes, above all the cause of sexual equality. In the history of ideas he has a star part. In furthering the legacy of the Enlightenment, in the development of a scientific approach to moral and social questions, he was a central figure of European significance. His influence upon contemporary and later positivism and radicalism was indisputable, even when that influence took the form of a reaction against him. He made much of his absorption and incorporation of the countercurrents of Romanticism and historism, and his dialectic between Enlightenment and Romanticism holds an enduring fascination, giving a unique insight into some of the intellectual dilemmas of his age. But here, the modern reader must take care not to be misled. Mill's incorporation of a historical, sociological and hermeneutic approach never went as far as he suggested; in spite of his claims, he failed to achieve a synthesis of the eighteenth and nineteenth centuries because he refused to accept some of the deeper insights of contemporary European (especially German) thought. Where the fundamentals were concerned, he remained closer to his father and Bentham than he was prepared to admit.

Apart from his place in our historical narratives, where does he stand in relation to us? Does he still matter, in the sense that we feel compelled to read him as if he were our contemporary, one with whom we must still debate and from whom we can learn? Some of the writings most esteemed in his own day are now of interest mainly to specialists. This is true of most of his *System of Logic*, and most of his *Principles of Political Economy*. The disciplines have moved on, and left his work behind. But if humans understand themselves and the world *contrastively*, grasping the theories they accept and endorse by contrasting them with contrary positions, even here Mill has a part to play in the self-understanding of modern minds. Some parts of both books are indisputably alive and kicking. The discussion of the human sciences in the last part of the *Logic* remains one of the most important treatments of this contentious and difficult topic. Mill's flexible, undogmatic approach to private property and taxation and his advocacy of a kind of market socialism have gained, or should have gained, a new lease of life in our postcommunist world.

Other writings have lost little of their relevance. With very few exceptions there is no dispute about the continuing importance of the essay *On Liberty*. Now that careless misreadings and arrogant misunderstandings have been cleared away, it is apparent that Mill's *Utilitarianism* contains a subtle and plausible moral philosophy, likely to survive as long as ethical discourse itself. *The Subjection of Women* will remain a classic feminist statement. His discussions of democracy, from 'The Spirit of the Age' to the *Considerations on Representative Government* offer intellectual refreshment to our age, in which lip service is all too often paid to the ideal, without thought about what it means.

In his last years, because of the range, power and perceived relevance of his thought, because of his contacts and influence in Britain, Europe, America and the colonies, Mill held a commanding position in the public eye. Since his death no mere intellectual has matched this in his native land. But was he, as he wrote of Armand Carrel, a hero of Plutarch in the modern world? Plutarch's Greek and Roman heroes are semi-mythical, most of them celebrated for killing many people or for their heroic deaths. Mill was a man of integrity and courage, but he killed no-one, was the victim of no more than a death-threat, and in his writings and correspondence left too full a picture of himself for myth-making to be possible.

SELECT BIBLIOGRAPHY

The bibliography below lists only those works to which reference is made in the text, but will serve the student as a guide to the most important ones. An almost complete bibliography of works on Mill in English can be found in Michael Laine (1982) *Bibliography of Works on John Stuart Mill*, Toronto and London: University of Toronto Press, and in *The Mill Newsletter*, 1965–89 succeeded by *Utilitas*, 1989 – .

Works by Mill

Reference is made to the complete edition, *Collected Works of John Stuart Mill*, ed. J.M. Robson and others, 33 vols, Toronto and London: University of Toronto Press. The form of referencing is as follows: (*CW*, vol. XXVIII, p. 358), and these are the volumes:

I (1980) *Autobiography and Literary Essays*
II, III (1965) *Principles of Political Economy*
IV, V (1967) *Essays on Economics and Society*
VI (1982) *Essays on England, Ireland and the Empire*
VII, VIII (1973) *System of Logic: Ratiocinative and Inductive*
IX (1979) *An Examination of Sir William Hamilton's Philosophy*
X (1969) *Essays on Ethics, Religion and Society*
XI (1978) *Essays on Philosophy and the Classics*
XII, XIII (1962) *Earlier Letters, 1812–1848*
XIV, XV, XVI, XVII (1972) *Later Letters, 1848–1873*
XVIII, XIX (1977) *Essays on Politics and Society*
XX (1985) *Essays on French History and Historians*
XXI (1984) *Essays on Equality, Law and Education*
XXII, XXIII, XXIV, XXV (1986) *Newspaper Writings*
XXVI, XXVII (1988) *Journals and Debating Speeches*
XXVIII, XXIX (1988) *Public and Parliamentary Speeches*
XXX (1990) *Writings on India*
XXXI (1989) *Miscellaneous Writings*
XXXII (1991) *Additional Letters*
XXXIII (1991) *Indexes*

Other works

Annan, N. (1969) 'John Stuart Mill', *Mill. A Collection of Critical Essays*, ed. Schneewind, J.B. London: Macmillan.

Annas, J. (1977) 'Mill and the Subjection of Women', *Philosophy*, 52, pp. 179–94.

Anschutz, R.P. (1953) *The Philosophy of J.S. Mill*, Oxford: Oxford University Press.

Arblaster, A. (1984) *The Rise and Decline of Western Liberalism*, Oxford: Blackwell.

Bain, A. (1882) *John Stuart Mill. A Criticism: with Personal Recollections*, London: Longmans, Green & Co.

Bentham, J. (1967) *A Fragment on Government and An Introduction to the Principles of Morals and Legislation*, Oxford: Blackwell.

Berger, F.R. (1984) *Happiness, Justice and Freedom: The Moral and Political Philosophy of John Stuart Mill*, Berkeley: University of California Press.

Berlin, I. (1969) *Four Essays on Liberty*, Oxford: Oxford University Press.

Bosanquet, B. (1923) *The Philosophical Theory of the State*, (1st edn, 1899), London: Macmillan.

Bradley, F.H. (1927) *Ethical Studies*, (1st edn, 1876), Oxford: Oxford University Press.

Brink, D.O. (1992) 'Mill's Deliberative Utilitarianism', *Philosophy and Public Affairs*, 21:1, pp. 67–103.

Burns, J.H. (1969) 'J. S. Mill and Democracy, 1829–1861', *Mill. A Collection of Critical Essays*, ed. Schneewind, J.B., London: Macmillan.

Burrow, J. (1988) *Whigs and Liberals. Continuity and Change in English Political Thought*, Oxford: Oxford University Press.

Caine, B. (1978) 'John Stuart Mill and the English Women's Movement', *Historical Studies*, 18, pp. 52–67.

Canovan, M. (1987) 'The Eloquence of John Stuart Mill', *History of Political Thought*, 8, pp. 505–20.

Carlisle, J. (1991) *John Stuart Mill and the Writing of Character*, Athens, Georgia: University of Georgia Press.

Coats, A.W. (1987) 'Samuel Hollander's Mill: A Review Article', *The Manchester School of Economic and Social Studies*, 55, pp. 310–16.

Collini, S. (1991) *Public Moralists. Political Thought and Intellectual Life in Britain*, Oxford: Oxford University Press.

Collini, S., Winch, D. & Burrow, J. (1983) *That Noble Science of Politics. A Study in Nineteenth-century Intellectual History*, Cambridge: Cambridge University Press.

Cowling, M. (1990) *Mill and Liberalism* (1st edn, 1963), Cambridge: Cambridge University Press.

Cumming, R.D. (1964) 'Mill's History of his Ideas', *Journal of the History of Ideas*, 25, pp. 235–56.

Devlin, P. (1965) *The Enforcement of Morals*, Oxford: Oxford University Press.

Dicey, A.V. (1914) *Lectures on the Relation between Law and Public Opinion in England During the Nineteenth Century* (2nd edn), London: Macmillan.

Donner, W. (1991) *The Liberal Self. John Stuart Mill's Moral and Political Philosophy*, Ithaca: Cornell University Press.

Donner, W. (1993) 'John Stuart Mill's Liberal Feminism', *Philosophical Studies*, 69, pp. 155–66.

Duncan, G. (1973) *Marx and Mill. Two Views of Social Conflict and Social Harmony*, Cambridge: Cambridge University Press.

Fox, C. (1882) *Memories of Old Friends* (2nd edn, 2 vols), London: Smith Elder & Co.

Francis, M. & Morrow, J. (1994) *A History of English Political Thought in the Nineteenth Century*, London: Duckworth.

Freeden, M. (1978) *The New Liberalism: An Ideology of Social Reform*, Oxford: Oxford University Press.

Friedman, R.B. (1969) 'An Introduction to Mill's Theory of Authority', *Mill. A Collection of Critical Essays*, ed. Schneewind, J.B., London: Macmillan.

Gilligan, C. (1982) *In a Different Voice*, Cambridge, Mass.: Harvard University Press.

Glassman, P.J. (1985) *J.S. Mill. The Evolution of a Genius*, Gainesville: University of Florida Press.

Gray, J. (1983) *Mill on Liberty: A Defence*, London: Routledge and Kegan Paul.

Gray, J. & Smith, G.W. (1991) *J.S. Mill On Liberty in Focus*, London: Routledge.

Hall, C. (1992) *White, Male and Middle Class*, Cambridge: Polity Press.

Hall, E.W. (1969) 'The "Proof" of Utility in Bentham and Mill' (originally published 1949), *Mill. A Collection of Critical Essays*, ed. Schneewind, J.B., London: Macmillan.

Halliday, R.J. (1976) *John Stuart Mill*, London: George Allen & Unwin.

Hamburger, J. (1976) 'Mill and Tocqueville on Liberty', *James and John Stuart Mill. Papers of the Centenary Conference*, eds Robson, J.M. and Laine, M., Toronto: University of Toronto Press.

Hamburger, J. (1989) Review of Burrow, *Whigs and Liberals*, *Utilitas*, 1:2, November, pp. 300–5.

Hampsher-Monk, I. (1992) *A History of Modern Political Thought*, Oxford: Blackwell.

Hart, H.L.A. (1963) *Law, Liberty and Morality*, Oxford: Oxford University Press.

Harvie, C. (1976) *The Lights of Liberalism. University Liberals and the Challenge of Democracy 1860–86*, London: Allen Lane.

Hayek, F.A. (1951) *John Stuart Mill and Harriet Taylor*, London: Routledge & Kegan Paul.

Hayward, A. (1873a) 'John Stuart Mill', *The Times*, 10 May, p. 5.

Hayward, A. (1873b) 'John Stuart Mill', *Fraser's Magazine*, NS 8, pp. 663–81.

Himmelfarb, G. (1974) *On Liberty and Liberalism. The Case of John Stuart Mill*, New York: Alfred A. Knopf.

Himmelfarb, G. (ed.) (1962) John Stuart Mill, *Essays on Politics and Culture*, New York: Doubleday.

Hoag, R.W. (1992) 'J.S. Mill's Language of Pleasures', *Utilitas*, 4:2, pp. 247–78.

Hollander, S. (1985) *The Economics of John Stuart Mill*, Oxford: Blackwell.

Honderich, T. (1982) '"On Liberty" and Morality-Dependent Harms', *Political Studies*, 30:4, pp. 504–14.

Jevons, S. (1871) *Theory of Political Economy*, London: Macmillan.

Jevons, S. (1890) *Pure Logic and Other Minor Works*, London: Macmillan.

Jones, E. (1953) *Sigmund Freud: Life and Works*, 2 vols, London: Hogarth Press.

Kendall, W. (1975) 'The "Open Society" and its Fallacies', *On Liberty*, ed. Spitz, D., New York: W.W. Norton & Co.

Kent, C. (1978) *Brains and Numbers: Elitism, Comtism and Democracy in Mid-Victorian Britain*, Toronto: University of Toronto Press.

Kinzer, B.L., Robson, A.P. & Robson, J.M. (1992) *A Moralist in and out of Parliament. John Stuart Mill at Westminster 1865–1868*, Toronto: University of Toronto Press.

Knights, B. (1978) *The Idea of the Clerisy in the Nineteenth Century*, Cambridge: Cambridge University Press.

Kurer, O. (1991a) *John Stuart Mill: The Politics of Progress*, New York & London: Garland.

Kurer, O. (1991b) 'John Stuart Mill and the Welfare State', *History of Political Economy*, 23:4, pp. 713–30.

Kurer, O. (1992) 'J. S. Mill and Utopian Socialism', *The Economic Record*, 68, pp. 222–32.

Letwin, S.R. (1965) *The Pursuit of Certainty. David Hume, Jeremy Bentham, John Stuart Mill, Beatrice Webb*, Cambridge: Cambridge University Press.

Lively, J. & Rees, J. (1978) *Utilitarian Logic and Politics*, Oxford: Oxford University Press.

Lyons, D. (1994) *Rights, Welfare and Mill's Moral Theory*, Oxford: Oxford University Press.

McCloskey, H.J. (1971) *John Stuart Mill: A Critical Study*, London: Macmillan.

Macpherson, C.B. (1977) *The Life and Times of Liberal Democracy*, Oxford: Oxford University Press.

Majeed, J. (1996) Review of Zastoupil, *John Stuart Mill and India*, *Utilitas*, 8, pp. 258–60.

Mazlish, B. (1975) *James and John Stuart Mill: Father and Son in the Nineteenth Century*, New York: Basic Books.

Mendus, S. (1989) 'The Marriage of True Minds: The Ideal of Marriage in the Philosophy of John Stuart Mill', *Sexuality and Subordination: Interdisciplinary Studies of Gender in the Nineteenth Century*, eds Mendus, S. & Rendall, J., London: Routledge.

Mendus, S. (1994) 'John Stuart Mill and Harriet Taylor on Women and Marriage', *Utilitas*, 6:2, pp. 287–99.

Moore, G.E. (1903) *Principia Ethica*, Cambridge: Cambridge University Press.

Moore, R.J. (1983) 'John Stuart Mill at East India House', *Historical Studies*, 20, pp. 497–519.

O'Brien, D.P. (1975) *The Classical Economists*, Oxford: Oxford University Press.

O'Grady, J. (1991) '"Congenial vocation": J.M. Robson and the Mill Project', *A Cultivated Mind: Essays on J.S. Mill Presented to John M. Robson*, ed. Laine, M., Toronto: University of Toronto Press.

Offen, K. (1988) 'Defining Feminism: a Comparative Historical Approach', *Signs: Journal of Women in Culture and Society*, 14:1, pp. 119–157.

Okin, S.M. (1979) *Women in Western Political Thought*, Princeton: Princeton University Press.

Packe, M. St.J. (1954) *The Life of John Stuart Mill*, London: Secker & Warburg.

Pappe, H.O. (1960) *John Stuart Mill and the Harriet Taylor Myth*, Cambridge: Cambridge University Press.

Plamenatz, J.P. (1958) *The English Utilitarians*, (1st edn, 1949) Oxford: Blackwell.

Pocock, J.G.A. (1975) *The Machiavellian Moment*, Princeton, N.J.: Princeton University Press.

Pyle, A. (ed.) (1994) *Liberty. Contemporary Responses to John Stuart Mill*, Bristol: Thoemmes Press.

Pyle, A. (ed.) (1995) *The Subjection of Women. Contemporary Responses to John Stuart Mill*, Bristol: Thoemmes Press.

Rees, J.C. (1960) 'A Re-reading of Mill on Liberty', *Political Studies*, 8, pp. 113–29.

Rees, J.C. (1985) *John Stuart Mill's On Liberty. Constructed from Published and Unpublished Sources by G.L. Williams*, Oxford: Clarendon Press.

Riley, J. (1996) 'J. S. Mill's Liberal Utilitarian Assessment of Capitalism versus Socialism', *Utilitas*, 8:1, pp. 39–71.

Robson, J.M. (1968) *The Improvement of Mankind. The Social and Political Thought of John Stuart Mill*, London: Routledge & Kegan Paul.

Robson, J.M. (1976) 'Rational Animals and Others', *James and John Stuart Mill. Papers of the Centenary Conference*, eds Robson, J.M. and Laine, M., Toronto: University of Toronto Press.

Rossi, A.S. (ed.) (1970) *J.S. Mill, Essays on Sex Equality*, Chicago: University of Chicago Press.

Russell, B. (1969) 'John Stuart Mill' (originally published 1951), *Mill. A Collection of Critical Essays*, ed. Schneewind, J.B., London: Macmillan.

Ryan, A. (1970) *The Philosophy of John Stuart Mill*, London: Macmillan.

Ryan, A. (1974) *J.S. Mill*, London: Routledge.

Ryan, A. (1991a) 'Sense and Sensibility in Mill's Political Thought', *A Cultivated Mind: Essays on J.S. Mill presented to John M. Robson*, ed. Laine, M., Toronto: University of Toronto Press.

Ryan, A. (1991b) 'John Stuart Mill's Art of Living', Gray, J. & Smith, G.W., *J.S. Mill On Liberty in Focus*, London: Routledge.

Schneewind, J.B. (1976) 'Concerning Some Criticisms of Mill's Utilitarianism, 1861–76', *James and John Stuart Mill. Papers of the Centenary Conference*, eds Robson, J.M. and Laine, M., Toronto: University of Toronto Press.

Schwarz, P. (1968) *The New Political Economy of J.S. Mill*, London: Weidenfeld & Nicholson.

Semmel, B. (1962) *The Governor Eyre Controversy*, London: MacGibbon & Kee.

Shanley, M.L. (1991) 'Marital Slavery and Friendship: John Stuart Mill's "The Subjection of Women"', *Feminist Interpretations and Political Theory*, eds Shanley, M.L. & Pateman, C., Cambridge: Polity Press.

Skorupski, J. (1989) *John Stuart Mill*, London: Routledge.

Soper, K. (ed.) (1983) *Harriet Taylor Mill, Enfranchisement of Women & John Stuart Mill, The Subjection of Women*, London: Virago.

Stephen, J.F. (1967) *Liberty, Equality, Fraternity* (1st edn, 1873), Cambridge: Cambridge University Press.

Stephen, L. (1912) *The English Utilitarians*, vol. III, *John Stuart Mill* (1st edn, 1900), London: Duckworth & Co.

Stigler, G.J. (1976) 'The Scientific Uses of Scientific Biography, with Special Reference to J.S. Mill', *James and John Stuart Mill. Papers of the Centenary Conference*, eds Robson, J.M. & Laine, M., Toronto: University of Toronto Press.

148   Select Bibliography

Stillinger, J. (1991) 'John Mill's Education: Fact, Fiction, and Myth', *A Cultivated Mind: Essays on J.S. Mill Presented to John M. Robson*, ed. Laine, M., Toronto: University of Toronto Press.

Stove, D. (1993) 'The Subjection of John Stuart Mill', *Philosophy*, 68, pp. 5–13.

Sullivan, E.P. (1983) 'Liberalism and Imperialism: J.S. Mill's Defense of the British Empire', *Journal of the History of Ideas*, 44:4, pp. 599–617.

Ten, C.L. (1980) *Mill on Liberty*, Oxford: Oxford University Press.

Thomas, W. (1979) *The Philosophic Radicals: Nine Studies in Theory and Practice 1817–1841*, Oxford: Oxford University Press.

Thomas, W. (1985) *Mill*, Oxford: Oxford University Press.

Tulloch, G. (1989) *Mill and Sexual Equality*, Hemel Hempstead: Harvester Wheatsheaf.

Urbinati, N. (1991) 'John Stuart Mill on Androgyny and Ideal Marriage', *Political Theory*, 19:4, pp. 626–48.

Urmson, J.O. (1969) 'The Interpretation of the Moral Philosophy of J.S. Mill' (originally published 1953), *Mill. A Collection of Critical Essays*, ed. Schneewind, J.B., London: Macmillan.

Walker, A.D.M. (1974) 'Negative Utilitarianism', *Mind*, 83, pp. 424–8.

Warnock, M. (1969) 'On Moore's Criticisms of Mill's "Proof"', *Mill. A Collection of Critical Essays*, ed. Schneewind, J.B., London: Macmillan.

Willey, B. (1964) *Nineteenth-Century Studies*, (1st edn, 1949) Harmondsworth: Penguin.

Williams, R. (1963) *Culture and Society 1780–1950*, Harmondsworth: Penguin.

Wilson, F. (1990) *Psychological Analysis and the Philosophy of John Stuart Mill*, Toronto: University of Toronto Press.

Winch, P. (1963, first published 1958) *The Idea of a Social Science and its Relation to Philosophy*, London: Routledge & Kegan Paul.

Wolfe, W. (1975) *From Radicalism to Socialism. Men and Ideas in the Formation of Fabian Socialist Doctrines, 1881–1889*, London and New Haven: Yale University Press.

Zastoupil, L. (1994) *John Stuart Mill and India*, Stanford: Stanford University Press.

Zimmer, L.B. (1976) 'John Stuart Mill and Democracy, 1866–7', *Mill Newsletter*, 11, pp. 3–17.

INDEX